Innovations in Education Series
Edited by Robert J. Brown

1. Edward J. Dirkswager, editor. *Teachers as Owners: A Key to Revitalizing Public Education.* 2002.
2. Darlene Leiding. *The Won't Learners: An Answer to Their Cry.* 2002.
3. Ronald J. Newell. *Passion for Learning: How Project-Based Learning Meets the Needs of 21st-Century Students.* 2003.

Passion for Learning

How Project-Based Learning Meets the Needs of 21st-Century Students

Ronald J. Newell

Innovations in Education Series, No.3
Edited by Robert J. Brown

Rowman & Littlefield Education
Lanham • New York • Toronto • Oxford
2003

This title was originally published by ScarecrowEducation.
First Rowman & Littlefield Education edition 2006.

Published in the United States of America
by Rowman & Littlefield Education
A Division of Rowman & Littlefield Publishers, Inc.
A wholly owned subsidiary of The Rowman & Littlefield Publishing Group, Inc.
4501 Forbes Boulevard, Suite 200, Lanham, Maryland 20706
www.rowmaneducation.com

PO Box 317
Oxford
OX2 9RU, UK

British Library Cataloguing in Publication Information Available

Library of Congress Cataloging-in-Publication Data

Newell, Ronald J.
  Passion for learning : how project-based learning meets the needs of
21st-century students / Ronald J. Newell.
      p. cm.—(Innovations in education series, no. 3)
"A ScarecrowEducation book."
Includes bibliographical references and index.
  ISBN 0-8108-4601-2 (pbk. : alk. paper)
  1. Project method in teaching—Minnesota—Henderson—Case studies. 2.
Education, Secondary—Minnesota—Henderson—Case studies. 3.
Individualized instruction—Minnesota—Henderson—Case studies. 4.
Minnesota New Country School (Henderson, Minn.)—Case studies. I.
Title. II. Innovations in education (Lanham, Md.) ; no. 3.
  LB1027.43 .N48 2003
  371.3'6—dc21   2002012021

⊗™ The paper used in this publication meets the minimum requirements of
American National Standard for Information Sciences—Permanence of
Paper for Printed Library Materials, ANSI/NISO Z39.48-1992.
Manufactured in the United States of America.

Contents

Foreword

Why do educators need to read yet one more book about high schools? What's the "problem" this book looks to solve?

Districts are making progress with elementary school reforms around the country. Fourth-grade reading and math scores are up in many states. In elementary schools where recently I've spent time, there's a sense of emergent pride and hope. Not so in secondary schools. Districts that have seen test scores increase for elementary age children see those same kids' scores fall in 8th grade. The slump is often even worse by the time the students get to the 10th grade. Secondary school reformers are profoundly demoralized. They have no sense of what's going wrong, or what new strategies they might try.

What is little understood is that the change challenge is profoundly different in elementary versus secondary education. To understand the differences, I'd like to suggest a three-part lens for analyzing successful improvements in teaching, curriculum, and school structure. They are the interdependent principles of *rigor*, *relevance*, and *relationships*. These lenses can also serve as useful guideposts for the reader of *Passion for Learning*.

Profound changes in our society over the last quarter century and the rapid shift from a blue-collar industrial economy to a knowledge economy means that all students now need new skills for work, citizenship, and college readiness. All students need a rigorous curriculum, but rigor is often interpreted to mean simply covering more of the same old tired traditional academic content. The problem with "more of the same" rigor is that the content is often irrelevant to many of today's students.

The traditional college-prep, lecture-style curriculum is not connected to the world from which many students come, nor does it align with the worlds for which students must be prepared.

Increasingly, all students must learn to reason, communicate, problem-solve, and work collaboratively, as Ron Newell points out. The skills now needed for work, college, and active, informed citizenship are essentially the same, but they are often not the skills being taught in many so-called "college prep curricula." Employers and professors agree that communications and study skills, good work habits, curiosity, and respect are what's most lacking among the nation's high school graduates, according to Public Agenda Foundation studies (see "Reality Check, 2002" at www.publicagenda.org). Except for basic math skills, neither group is concerned about lack of proficiency in traditional academic disciplines.

Rigor as a curriculum concept must be connected to relevance. Early in the 20th century, we gave up teaching Greek and Latin as required courses in high school for a reason—mastery of these languages was no longer considered essential. Yet we have not really reconsidered the "Carnegie unit" as a framework for thinking about what students need to know in high school since its inception in 1906. We now need to better connect today's secondary school curriculum to the interests and needs of the students we teach, as well as to the skills they'll need as adults.

Such curricula exists in many highly successful secondary schools that use what I call a "merit badge" approach as a way for students to rigorously demonstrate mastery of core competencies. Minnesota New Country School, the focal point of Ron Newell's book, was an early leader in the development of this approach and has had dramatic successes with its students. Even inner-city schools that have developed similar approaches to teaching and learning find that more than 90 percent of their students graduate; of those, more than 90 percent go on to two- and four-year colleges, in contrast to traditional high schools serving the same populations, where fewer than 50 percent of the students graduate.

But Rigor and Relevance aren't the only explanations for the successes of Minnesota New Country and the "reinvented" high schools in New York and elsewhere. They are also built on the principle of establishing and maintaining strong *relationships* between students and adults who care and are knowledgeable about what students are learning. In focus groups of today's adolescents, I have found that the students' persistent complaint about school is that "no one cares." Even students in advanced placement courses tell me that adults seem too busy to listen to them. Growing up in single parent or dual career families, today's students have much less of an adult presence in their lives. They need connections to caring adults in order to be *motivated* to master an academically rigorous, relevant curriculum.

Good elementary schools, where students spend most of their day with the same teacher, have always been built around caring *relationships*. Introducing *rigor* and *relevance* has involved curriculum and professional development challenges, but the nature of the changes are comparatively modest. Reading has to be more focused around material that students want to read, and teachers have to learn how to raise expectations for all students. The elementary "scope of work" is reform, not reinvention. The changes required do not challenge teachers' and parents' conceptions of school. We have known what good elementary school classrooms look like for some time. The challenge is replicating it at scale, and few have to be convinced of the need. Most people understand the importance of all children learning to read and to do math.

In order to succeed with all students in middle and high school, however, we have to go back to the drawing board and "reinvent" secondary education. We must challenge many academics' notions of what constitutes a "rigorous" curriculum and create a course of study that is as relevant as it is rigorous. We need to bring the kinds of skills mentioned in the 1991 SCANS report into the core content of our academic courses. We might even want to consider teaching courses around modes of problem-solving rather than by the traditional academic Carnegie unit compartmentalization. Above all, we must create small school communities, or what I call *new village schools*, where caring adults are much more knowledgeable about and involved with all students' learning.

Ron and his colleagues who work at Minnesota New Country are pioneers in this reinvention process and they have blazed a vivid trail. This book is an invaluable guide and resource for those who are just undertaking the journey. It is must reading for anyone who wants to know more about how our nation's secondary schools can be dramatically improved. *Passion for Learning* demonstrates in a very concrete manner the importance and interdependency of *rigor*, *relevance*, and *relationships* as three core principles for redesigning our nation's public schools.

Tony Wagner
Codirector of the Change Leadership Group
at the Harvard Graduate School of Education
www.newvillageschools.org

Preface

The twentieth-century education system was noted for developing a method that helped fulfill the American dream for millions of people. It did so by adopting measures and policies that allowed for many foreign born peoples to learn a culture and a language of commerce that helped forge a nation of doers and, to some degree, thinkers. It did so by creating a factory-like model that brought high school age children into one place where libraries and experts could be gathered to impart information to their young people. Yet the education system that helped America become the dynamic way of life it had become was slowly dying as the twentieth century came to a close. Many would argue that the system itself had become too large, schools too big for the closeness needed to foster the passion for learning that the nation's people supposedly had developed over the first half of the last century

Schools, especially high schools, by the end of the twentieth century were simply not doing the job as well as they seemingly had since the middle of the century. Businesses were complaining that a workforce was not well prepared. Colleges and universities claimed students came to them ill prepared for the rigors of academic life. Violent behavior in schools became prevalent in the news. Graduation rates, especially of large urban high schools, were woefully inadequate. Reform measures were attempted by the system for twenty years or more, many of them wishing to restore the smaller, more intimate settings of schooling in the first half of the century. But the reform measures were shunted aside by a bureaucratic system time after time, given short shrift over maintaining status quo, with millions of public and private dollars going to waste.

What was going on here? Perhaps the factory-model school, with the interchangeable parts, the assembly-line method of depositing information, was the culprit. The public was sold on a system that did not deliver upon its promise. We were told that if we built great cathedrals to learning, with beautiful tiled floors, large gymnasiums and swimming pools, with new desks and new books, with large numbers of specialists in various disciplines each in their own Shangri-la-like rooms, then education would be better and better. If only we could offer more courses! More AP courses! More specialties! More programs! More choices for our children! Then we would have a better school!

The large, shopping-mall schools that were sold to suburban and urban populations soon were sold to small rural communities. In order to afford them, they had to consolidate districts together so that a cathedral-like school building could be built in a nearby community. Soon, small rural towns lost their schools—the schools that allowed teachers to build relationships with students, allowed teachers to work independently with students, and allowed students to build relationships to their communities.

However, the Information Age's technological revolution made it possible to disseminate information in wholly new ways: computer programs, the Internet, videos and cable television programs all could deliver information to young and old while not in school. No longer was it necessary to bus children into the large, imposing buildings in larger communities, where the student soon lost the emotional intimacy once associated with the small elementary or small high school setting. It was possible, and probable, the passion for learning was something young people could develop more so outside of school than in school.

What is needed for the twenty-first century is a return to that small setting, a place where students were known, where they could build upon a passion for learning that is inherent in every three year old, where learning from outside sources was validated. Such a reform was initiated with the development of the Minnesota New Country School in 1994. It is a public charter school that developed a project-based system of learning, utilizing a personalized education for high school age students that allowed for a great deal of choice in accomplishing a high school education. This book is about that school and its program. It is a program that began to gain national attention in the late 1990s, culminating with a grant from the Bill & Melinda Gates Foundation in 2000 to replicate the model nationwide. That effort has had a good start, with seven schools utilizing the model in only one year after the grant. Many educators have visited the school to learn about its unusual education delivery system and the method of governing the school. What that model delivers is the topic of this book. A project-based system, where integrated projects are created around a set of state-established inquiry standards, can either keep alive a passion for learning, or revitalize a passion for learning lost due to matriculation in a large, unfriendly atmosphere.

Many would, perhaps, say at this juncture that such a school could only exist in a narrowly confined setting, that such a thing could not become the norm for the American education system. I disagree. It is possible to create neighborhood schools with 100–150 students in grades 7–12. They do not have to be only an aberration, a condition of the charter school movement. It will take courage on the part of community groups, parents, educators, and students to adopt a new way (or, shall I say an old way with new technologies) to educate young people.

The Gates-EdVisions Project has created six schools based upon the project-based learning program of the New Country School. Some are made up of learners in 7th–12th grade, some 9th–12th. Three of those are found in urban settings. Although all three are in their first year, and two of them are conversion schools, the promise of project-based learning has created a chance for urban youth to develop a personalized education with the help of adults as mentors. A model worth visiting, to see that urban young people can develop or maintain a passion for learning, is Avalon Charter School in St. Paul. Only in their first year, Avalon students already have developed a love for the setting, developed deep relationships with the advisor/teachers, and have developed some very interesting projects. It is not true that urban youth are too illiterate, too apathetic, or too difficult to educate in this manner.

This book was created to give heart to parents who know that the present system is not doing well by their children; to give heart to the small towns across America that they can keep their middle and high school age children in the community; and to give heart to urban educators who know that they need to connect their students to their passions in order to get meaningful learning.

Acknowledgments

There are many people without whom this work would not have been possible. To all of the advisors, who over the years helped develop the project-based process and assessment system, I thank you for the time and effort it took to create something from nothing. Most of all a large thank-you to Minnesota New Country advisors Dee Thomas, Dean Lind, GiGi Robosenski, Keven Kroehler, Anthony Sonnek, and Jeff Anderson for being the great advisors that you are. Also, a big thank-you to the support staff for their ongoing support of learners and the project process.

I also am grateful to Doug Thomas for his continued support and guidance for this project and to Mary Murphy and Pat Grapentine for their help. A large debt is also owed to the Bill & Melinda Gates Foundation for their support of the New Country model and for making it possible for the nation to build small, focused high schools based on student needs.

I would like to make a special acknowledgement to Dee Thomas for her leadership, commitment, and dedication to the project-based model. This was to be a joint project, but she was too busy with being the president of the Minnesota Association of Charter Schools and being on the Minnesota Board of Teaching as well as her duties at New Country. Her work with learners and educators is an inspiration to many.

I would also like to acknowledge my favorite editor and companion, my wife Caroljean, for her ongoing love and support in this project. A very heartfelt thank-you to all of you.

CHAPTER 1

What Is Project-Based Learning?

It is paradoxical that many educators and parents still differentiate between a time for learning and a time for play without seeing the vital connection between them.

—Leo Buscaglia

The Minnesota New Country School is a school without regularly scheduled classes, no classrooms, no bells, few textbooks, no teachers in front of a class, no large group instruction, and very few students doing the same activity at the same time. In short, it does not look like a typical school. How, then, does any learning take place? The best answer to that is to look at a couple of cases.

In a recent visit to the school, I briefly interviewed two students who were seemingly highly engaged. I asked Kacie, a 17-year-old senior, what has been the project she most enjoyed. Her response was "the history project on the Mayo House." LeSueur, Minnesota, Kacie's hometown, is the site of the early home of the young doctors Mayo, the founders of the world famous Mayo Clinic. The original home is now a museum. Kacie has served as a tour guide, having applied for the job and been hired. She did so because of her general interest in history and because her brother had worked there as a guide. She was very pleased to know that her work with the museum could be used in a project for school, where she would get credit toward meeting standards in the state-wide curriculum and hours toward meeting project credits.

Kacie "liked learning about medicine of the era," how "people lived in those circumstances in those times," and learned that she would have a "difficult time living like that." She also felt that her interaction with visitors, who asked a lot of questions she had to "think on her feet" to answer, was a positive experience for her. Older visitors liked to reminisce and she "learned a lot from the visitors" about life in the early part of the 20 century as well as the 19th century.

Her project called for her to have a product or a performance to show what she learned, so Kacie created a PowerPoint presentation giving a "virtual tour" of the Mayo House. The director of the museum is now using this PowerPoint presentation as a training tool for new guides. Kacie was very pleased to have made a useful contribution to the museum. As a result of the project, Kacie exhibited some level of mastery of state standards in aspects of American history, technology, and academic reading and writing.

Kacie's Senior Project, a project requiring three times as much time and effort as a regular project, is a spin-off of the Mayo House project. She is presently engaged in developing an "oral history" of the community of LeSueur. She has developed interview questions, interviewed a number of long-term residents, and will develop a publishable book for the project. Kacie said, "you have to think a lot about what you want when you choose people to interview and what you want to include." This project, she determined, will probably take her 400 hours or more to complete.

When asked what else she is involved in, Kacie mentioned that she is a PSEO student half time (Minnesota has a post-secondary option that allows high school students to attend college for both high school and college credits). She has taken French I and Astronomy at a local state university, and now is taking French II and Biology. She really enjoys the French classes and says they are "easier than she thought they would be." She took French because she "wanted to be different," as most high school students in the area attend Spanish or German classes.

When asked what are her aspirations after high school, Kacie thought she would major in English composition and writing, possibly taking some journalism classes. She is not interested so much in writing for newspapers, but in using it as a stepping stone to writing books. Kacie has a deep interest in writing and wants to make contributions to the world as a historical writer.

Barb, a 16 year old in her first year at the Minnesota New Country School, was working with creating clay "dolls" and equipment when I stopped by her work station. I asked what she was working on, and she said, "I am making a Claymation video of the Beach Boys 'Cocomo' song. These characters will be band members, and I have made a set of drums, a guitar, and sound equipment. It's really fun." She went on to explain that she will take digital still photos of the characters in poses and use Adobe Premiere, a computer program, to put them together in a film. When asked how she learned to use the computer program, she replied, "Keven (the advisor at the school with the most technology skill) showed me the basics, but I just learn as I go."

I asked Barb how she got such an idea, and she said that using clay and animation was something she was interested in from seeing movies like *Chicken Run* and from things she learned at a previous school. But, the circumstances at the other school did not allow her to pursue carrying out her dreams to the extent of actually creating a video. Barb said that the video will require her taking 20 stills for every second of video. The song is 3 minutes and 40 seconds in length, so she estimates it will take nearly 3000 still photos to complete the video.

What Barb would be able to accomplish in the state standards would include exhibiting a level of mastery of: arts (designing characters and settings, in creating a video, utilizing music); technology (using various creative programs); technical reading and writing (using computer manuals and explaining the process she uses); and some math (using proportions). Barb does not know for sure if these items are all that will be met, as she is in the middle of the project and new things could develop that she is unaware of at this time.

An offshoot of the project is learning how to play the guitar on her own from books she bought at a music store. And, she is presently doing a project on the history of the guitar. Along with that, she is learning the basics of photography—lighting, developing and other technical aspects. From that, she is learning about chemistry and physics.

With another student, Barb is finishing up the creation of a 15-minute video of the events of her 4-H Club. Using 800 pictures taken throughout the year, Barb and her friend have scanned the photos and used Adobe Premiere to put in voice-over and music to create the film. From her projects, which took place over less than one-half of a year at the school, Barb said she has "learned many computer programs I never even knew existed." She used books on the programs, some help from advisors at the school, but basically learned them on her own.

Barb was homeschooled for her first eight years of education. She then went to the local traditional high school for ninth grade. She said that while homeschooled, she had freedom in creating her work time and the curriculum. When she went to the high school, she was "told what to do all the time." She did not like classes, lectures, teachers in general (although she liked some), bells, lockers, and basically the whole atmosphere. Her brother and some friends had come to the New Country School, so she thought she would try it. "I really like it here. We have the freedom to choose how, when and what we want to study. It's fun."

The above two examples, only two snapshots of a possible 125 students in the school, should give the reader an idea of what project-based learning at the Minnesota New Country School is about. Other examples could be mentioned of engaging projects, as well: Denise and her establishing a Big Brother, Big Sister Program in the local community; Seth and his Solar System Project; or Chris and his Light Wave Project. Many interesting things are going on every day at the school.

In 1995 a group of New Country learners went on a field trip to a nearby nature center in order to find possibilities for biology and environmental projects. The group found a large number of deformed frogs. From that summer excursion came a large amount of publicity and projects for a number of students over time. Because this school was different, the find was placed on the school website. Because the learners could engage in their passion to learn when the need was perceived, the group wanted to pursue the deformed frogs to a logical conclusion. Department of Natural Resources personnel, university personnel, and students from New Country pursued the reasons for the deformities, causing the state legislature to fund research, often carried out by New Country students and staff. Six years of research was carried on by a large number of learners along with various agencies. Obviously, it is not school as usual.

The peculiar project-based system developed at the Minnesota New Country School is a product of seven years of trial and error, of action research by the staff, of continual engagement in staff development opportunities, and a commitment on part of the learning community at the school to provide the best possible personalized and authentic education to learners. It is necessary to know that this particular, unique project-based system is the total learning program at the school.

In other words, projects are not used as an aside to classroom instruction; are not used as thematic instruction; are not used as a way to provide some integration; are not used to give students some motivation to continue with their class work. Projects are the primary means by which learners graduate with a high school diploma. Projects are the means by which learners meet state-mandated standards. Projects are means by which learners learn basic skills. Projects are the means by which learners learn how to learn, learn about the world, learn who they are and what they want to become.

Project-based learning is a revolutionary way to learn, one that is much different from the traditional way high school students usually pursue an education (Buck Institute, 2001). Project-based learning emphasizes depth of understanding over content coverage; comprehension of concepts and principles rather than knowledge of facts; development of complex problem-solving skills rather than learning building block skills in isolation. Project-based learning emphasizes student interest rather than following a fixed curriculum; emphasizes a broad, interdisciplinary focus rather than a narrow, discipline-based focus; uses direct, primary, or original sources rather than texts, lectures, and secondary sources; emphasizes data and materials developed by students rather than by teachers.

Furthermore, project-based learning completely changes the role of the teacher: from lecturer and director of instruction to that of resource provider and participant in the learning activities; and from expert to advisor/facilitator. Assessment requires processes or performances and tangible accomplishments to be witnessed rather than products or tests, and demonstration of learning rather than reproduction of information.

Project-based learning also refocuses the usage of technology from an ancillary or peripheral use to a central and integral part of the process; from technology administered by teachers to technology directed by students; from technology useful for teacher presentations to technology enhancing student presentations.

The student role in project-based learning becomes one of carrying out self-directed learning activities rather than carrying out teacher-directed activities; defining their own roles, tasks, and time management rather than receiving and completing brief, directed tasks; learning how to communicate, show, affect, produce, and take responsibility rather than listen, behave, or speak only when spoken to. The short-term goals change from knowledge of facts, terms, and content to understanding and application of complex ideas and processes; from mastery of isolated skills to mastery of integrated skills. Long-term goals change from breadth of knowledge to depth of knowledge; from performing successfully on standard achievement tests to acquiring dispositions and skills to engage in sustained, lifelong learning.

It can hardly be disputed that the goals and emphases of project-based learning are excellent goals for the American student. The 1991 SCANS Report identified five competencies, with sub-competencies, for the high school graduate:

- Identifies, organizes, plans, and allocates resources; i.e., time management, money management, material and facilities management, human resources management.
- Works with others; i.e., participates as a member of a team, teaches others new skills, serves clients/customers, exercises leadership, negotiates, works with diversity.
- Acquires and uses information; i.e., acquires and evaluates information, organizes and maintains information, interprets and communicates information, uses computers to process information.
- Understands complex interrelationships; i.e., understands systems, monitors and corrects performance, improves or designs systems.
- Works with a variety of technologies; i.e., selects technology, applies technology to a task, maintains and troubleshoots equipment.

All of the above skills, although pronounced valid over a decade ago, are difficult to achieve in the traditional system, where a learner is a memorizer and repeater of facts; where brief, unconnected activities take place; where a learner has very little choice; and where there are very few long-term learning activities. Most typical activity in a traditional and "normal" high school will not deliver on the overall development of a young person on their journey to a productive and fulfilling adulthood. However, a purely project-based school, one that utilizes learning program technology that asks learners to devise, develop, process, self-assess, produce, and perform a long-term project can deliver on these important skills.

Take, for example, the snapshot of the two students from the Minnesota New Country School. Kacie's Mayo House history project helped her decide that she *wanted* to learn about the history of the late 19th century and early 20th century. Thereby she gained: a depth of understanding of life in those times; comprehension of concepts and principles pertaining to change and historical development; problem-solving and computer skills in creating a PowerPoint presentation; utilization of a broad, interdisciplinary focus on not only history, but medicine; the ability to obtain and develop data from primary sources, interviews, and documents; the ability to use technology as a central element in her work; the ability to carry out self-directed activities; how to go about synthesizing information; the ability to discover and present ideas; the ability to take responsibility for her work; an understanding of complex ideas and processes; and a capability of engaging in sustained, autonomous, lifelong skills.

These above-mentioned skills are closely interrelated to the SCANS skills, as can be readily seen. Kacie knows how to use resources, she has shown she can work with others, she certainly has acquired and applied knowledge, she understands complex interrelationships, and she has worked with a variety of technologies. In one project, Kacie has had to use skills that she will need in the "real world." And since she has had to do many projects, she has practiced the skills many times over.

More importantly, the comments and activities of Barb, the other student interviewed, show the real strength of project-based learning. Barb was actually having fun! Imagine that. Having fun at high school and not playing a game or teasing fellow students! The power isn't only in the outcomes of project-based learning, although they are very important; the power is in the *intrinsic motivation* provided by the method. When students can have a choice of topic, have time to really investigate something of interest, can be given responsibility, and can see an authentic (at least to them) goal and rationale, intrinsic motivation and a heightened sense of alertness and interest becomes a natural by-product. This intrinsic motivation keeps students in school, keeps them enthused, and keeps them happy. Therefore, the *door of opportunity* is opened to learning worthwhile, meaningful skills. Although it can be said that the large comprehensive high school has hundreds of offerings, skilled and knowledgeable experts in every classroom, and a curriculum so fine-tuned as to be considered impeccable, learners will not learn if they are not *motivated*! It is not enough to motivate by grades, by fear of not graduating, by intimidation, or by detention and suspensions. Those things do not open the door of learning opportunities; rather they deter meaningful learning.

The point is that motivation is increased on the part of the learner because project-based learning offers a number of distinct advantages. *Life-long learning* skills are an obvious outcome, and can be explained to learners and their parents. It is an instant buy-in. Project-based learning can be *learner-driven learning*, catering to the needs and interests of the students. Allowing choice builds intrinsic motivation and learning becomes natural and meaningful. It is also *just-in-time learning*, recognizing that the best learning opportunities are created when the learner is interested in them.

There is a maxim I learned to live with many years ago, as a classroom teacher, and reinforced when teaching at the New Country School: *people learn what they need to learn when they perceive they need to learn it*! No amount of struggle by teachers will force learners to learn what we perceive is necessary for them, until they see the need for that knowledge or skill. We can become expert at explaining the need for our subject matter, or we can learn all kinds of "class management skills" to coerce learners to learn what we want them to learn. But, in the end, they grasp and retain what they find important to them. And they certainly do not apply anything until they see where in their real world it is useful and meaningful, where it adds value to their lives.

Project-based learning also can be *customized learning*. Because New Country students have a choice as to how they are going to validate learning of standards, a project may be customized to that person's interests and strengths, but also can be tailored to a person's weaknesses and needs. Because students can use technology or not, can choose topics, can choose which of their particular "intelligences" to use in producing a product, projects become very customized.

Project-based learning can also be *collaborative learning*, where individual learning can be shifted away from the individual to small group, large group, or community activity. Many of the learners at the New Country School do projects within and for the community, and all are encouraged to do community service projects at some point in their matriculation.

Through the project process, New Country students are encouraged to contact outside experts whenever possible. Doing their projects with community experts in the real world of occupations allows for *contextual learning*, where learning is relevant to the expectations of the learner because it is occurring in context of the event. The projects allow for learning to make sense, heightening alertness and intrinsic motivation.

Project-based learning also allows for *learning-to-learn skills* to become habitual, so learners may learn what they need to learn when they need to learn it. This, then, makes project-based learning the primary means by which truly *transformational learning* can take place. For years the educational establishment has been saying it is about transforming society, but has shown very little evidence for having created situations where graduates have actually been developing the skills to transform themselves and their society. However, with skills gained from the project-based approach, learners can actually see themselves making a difference in their world, making it possible for them to make the commitment to transform their attitudes and beliefs and aspire to higher expectations for self and society.

Project-based learning has always held great promise for educators. All that was needed was a way to make it a reality. That is what the designers and practitioners of the Minnesota New Country School set out to do. The following pages will describe the methods they have created, some examples of how projects were created, and the process of assessment. But first, more about the theory of learning that led to the development of a purely project-based method.

CHAPTER 2

What Is Learning?

Understanding is not an acquisition that clicks into place at a certain developmental juncture . . . processes of understanding involve sets of performances—carrying out analyses, making fine judgements, undertaking syntheses, and creating products that embody principles or concepts central to a discipline.

—Howard Gardner

In much of the literature written about education reform, very little has been said about what *learning* is. It is as if everyone knows exactly what it means to learn and that all persons know what it is that has been learned. Nothing can be farther from the truth. With the dissemination of brain research details, it has become increasingly clear that most of the discussion skirts the issue; just what do we mean when we say someone has learned something?

The discussion on state and national "learning" standards has raised questions about the difference between behavioral objectives and competencies. Do we really know what is the difference? Professional educators often differ in their views, thereby creating confusion amongst the public. Not only is it confusing, but by creating objectives and competency standards educators have in effect made it unnecessary for parents and students to construct their own learning objectives. When students and parents are removed from the process we have what David Matthews (1997) calls a lack of legitimacy and loss of public trust. The people, and the students, don't feel as if the school is theirs. When are parents and students allowed to set standards for themselves? More importantly, when are parents and students going to be allowed to decide what *learning* is?

When the word *choice* is attached to school, rarely does it mean student choice of what they want to learn, and rarely are they asked what they understand by having "learned." John Dewey insisted on the participation of the learner in the formation of the purposes for their own learning. In a democratic country, we have often said that we believe in the participation of the governed. Should it not be necessary to allow all constituents to participate in the discussion on what is important to learn? Perhaps the parents and students ought to be involved in the discussion on what learning means? A non-educator's view of the nature of learning may very well be in order.

When in doubt, consult a dictionary (one of those lifelong learning skills everyone writes about!); Webster's defines learning as "1) acquisition of knowledge or skill, and 2) knowledge or skill acquired by instruction or study." The word *acquire* has some interest. It is defined as "to gain, by any means, usually by one's own exertions." It comes from the Latin *ad+quaerere*, to seek. In other words, learning is seeking out knowledge and skill, and by our efforts making it our own.

There is a comfort in discovering the meanings of words. When the words were first devised, they were done so because there was a particular action to describe. Our present culture has the same actions to describe, and by discovering what previous generations devised, we make our own actions clearer.

With this in mind, let us also take into account the word *pedagogy*. It comes from two Greek words, *paidos* + *agogos*, meaning "child leader," "leader of children." If teaching is pedagogy, leading of children, and learning is "seeking out knowledge and skills," which is determined primarily by the efforts of the learner, then teaching could be looked upon as the leading of children down a path, somewhat known to the leader, toward a predetermined goal. This creates an image of learning as a *journey* one takes to discover and acquire useful knowledge and skills, a journey accompanied by a "leader" of sorts.

And where is the journey going? Where ought the children to go? The end result would appear to be a useful adulthood. Who determines what is a useful adulthood? There are four forces that should determine the goal of the journey: one, society at large, or the political/economic

leaders of the nation-state; two, education leaders, professional pedagogues, who have been over the path before and have studied it; three,
the parents of the children; and four, the children themselves. No one
of the four is greater than the other. Yes, I realize that children at young
ages should not make all decisions for themselves, but they ought to
have a say in those decisions, and, as they grow older, make more and
more of them. And parents ought to be listened to, as they are the ones
who have brought the children into the world with an idea of what they
wanted them to become. If their idea of what the journey ought to look
like differs from the leaders of the state and the professional pedagogues, then the leaders and professionals ought to listen and take into
account those wishes.

The leaders of the nation-state and the professional educators have a
major role in the journey, which is primarily creating an infrastructure
for the journey and preparing leaders for the next generation of children. Because this costs taxpayers a great deal of money, money the
leaders have expropriated from the taxpayers for this purpose, the leaders believe they have the right to make all the decisions. But, the taxpayers have been making statements about what they think ought to be
done as well, and the taxpayers are also the parents. Parents appear to
want choices for their children, which is in keeping with the tenants of
our free country. Children need to learn to make wise decisions in a free
democracy, one with an open society that has a great deal of information and scintillation to offer youth. Parents also are "pedagogues" in
the sense of being leaders of their children in making wise decisions.

We must trust the professional leader/pedagogue to lead in the right
direction, the direction that is co-developed by the four forces. The role
of society and the infrastructure is to help develop good pedagogues
who can be trusted to lead children according to the wishes of the society, the parents, and the child. This takes a skillful pedagogue, who
understands how children learn, how society can be a part of the journey, and how to include both parental and learner choices. And, they
will know how to "assess" the journey (more about this in chapter 3).

First, it is necessary to listen to the professional pedagogues, those
who have taken and studied the long journey. What they have been
saying, as a result of recent brain research, is that humans learn best:
when they engage the limbic system (emotions); when they connect

new events with old events and see patterns in those events (creating a deep meaning); when there is an authentic task that has an immediate or near immediate result; and when the activity allows them some choice in the matter. Again, using the journey analogy, when learners have a choice of what path to take, when they have a stake in moving along that path, when they can see how this path is similar and different from other paths, and when they see a real reason for taking that particular path, then they will learn about taking paths in general and will realize a goal at the end of the path (if there, indeed, ever is an end to it).

What the learner may *acquire* along this path are: the skills of negotiating paths in general; learning to use resources (such as utilizing the knowledge of others who have been over the path and learning to use particular equipment that helps them negotiate paths); learning to overcome obstacles; learning to enjoy the aesthetic beauty of the surroundings; learning that it is worth working hard to get to a worthwhile destination; and learning how to apply what they learned on that path when they take a new one.

What does it take to negotiate the path to adulthood? Professional pedagogues would say that it takes good communication skills (reading, writing), mathematical aptitude and skill, an understanding of how the world works scientifically, an understanding of how human beings interact with each other, how to care for oneself and the environment, and possibly some skills and/or appreciation of the arts, in order to enjoy the journey more.

I believe the whole standards movement may be summed up in the above two paragraphs. Unfortunately, there is much controversy over what are the skills necessary to accomplish the journey, and to what degree must they be known. This is why there is a difficulty with the concept of what *learning* is. Some professional pedagogues would insist upon knowledge of thousands of content-oriented behavioral objectives (perhaps more because of job protection than any other reason). Some believe that all persons need the exact same skills, that all objectives need to be standardized (hence the standards movement), while others believe that each individual may possess different skills. This problem has caused all sorts of difficulty in the education system in the past couple of decades.

In the first place, the traditional system has since the beginning of the 20th century retained the concept of behaviorism (think Pavlov's dogs), that basically says people learn essential skills by repetition, by a system of rewards and/or punishments. Recent brain research has shown that behaviorism only works for "low level" learning, such as for survival, "fight or flight" skills, for basic animal instincts. But fear of punishment and repetition do not work when considering "high level" thinking, for skills like problem-solving, critical thinking, creativity, and abstraction. If regurgitation of bits of content is the ultimate goal, then perhaps a behaviorist approach makes some sense. And this is where most high schools are stuck—still dealing out content-oriented behavioral objectives that are not conducive to learning skills for the modern world.

Damasio, as discussed by Sylwester (2000b), has shown that the *core consciousness* manages internal mechanisms, which continually explore the constantly fluctuating external environment. "Sensory and related brain systems provide a mechanism for mapping and connecting the external world. The mapped relationships produce a nonverbal *feeling* of what is currently happening. Feelings, then, activate consciousness" (p. 22). Core consciousness is an "imaged and nonverbal account of objects an organism continually confronts" (p. 22). *Extended consciousness*, which requires a large frontal cortex, is the ability to develop an autobiographical memory allowing for movement from past to future, identifying a large possible range of information to apply to a novel event. This extended consciousness is the root of intelligence, which has as practical applications such things as imagination, creativity, and conscience. These, according to Sylwester, "lead to language, art, science, technology, and a variety of cultural and political systems"(p. 22).

To put it more simply: what causes humans to "extend" their consciousness (learn? acquire knowledge and skills?) is engagement of the emotion through sensory input, which leads to imagination, creativity, and conscience, which leads to skill development in communication, math and science, technology, social understanding, and the arts. If this is indeed true, then behaviorist theories that ask learners to do repetitive tasks to learn low level skills and bits of content in a punish/reward system are counterproductive to learning higher level skills, even communication, understanding of science and math, social studies and technology.

Hart (2002) and Caine & Caine (1994) refer to the "downshifting" mechanism that the brain uses when it is threatened, which causes learners to put into gear there "fight or flight" emotions, which for all practical purposes shuts off the frontal cortex from "extending consciousness."

Caine & Caine (1994) speak of the difference between acquisition of information and acquisition of meaning. When meaningfulness is ignored, real learning has not actually taken place. One soon forgets information after acquisition if there is no attachment to previous concepts of the world, or if the information does not connect on a deeper level. What we have in most high schools is an "extreme emphasis on *surface knowledge*, which is basically content void of significance to the learner" (Caine & Caine, 1994, p. 101). Deeper, *felt meaning* (described by Caine & Caine as the "aha" experience), is motivational and connecting, and happens when an emotional attachment has taken place. When learners are engaged in deeply felt and meaningful experiences, challenging activities are joyful and absorbing. This joyfulness and absorption certainly were evident in the two students, Kacie and Barb, highlighted in the last chapter.

Therefore, what is often considered learning, acquiring bits and pieces of information and low level skills, that are often the subjects of standardized tests and of basic curriculums everywhere, is *not* real learning! Even Einstein believes that: "Imagination is more important than knowledge. For knowledge is limited, whereas imagination embraces the entire world, stimulates progress, giving birth to evolution" (quoted in Wagmeister & Shifrin, 2000, p. 48).

Another misconception about learning is that those bits and pieces of information are inviolate and cannot be questioned. The basic give and take in schools is that the teacher says what is true, and the student must accept and memorize that fact. There is little credence given to student inquiry or questioning. This often pits student against teacher in an antagonistic approach—*you will believe that I am correct, you will learn what I tell you is important, and I will "grade" you down if you do not.* Which is a pretty good way to develop "downshifting" to lower brain activity and little learning at all.

According to Yoram and Lefstein (2000, p. 54), "the ability to pose questions to understand ourselves and our world is at the heart of what it means to be human. Unfortunately, this essential human trait is distorted in many schools by what we term the 'answering pedagogy.' In an answering pedagogy, answers largely eclipse the questions." Questioning is the means by which humans develop the core consciousness and allows movement toward the extended consciousness necessary for higher level learning. "In a questioning pedagogy, good questions do not indicate a deficiency; rather they reveal involvement in and a deep understanding of the subject. Good questions indicate an active, critical, and creative attitude toward knowledge" (p. 54). Questioning is the epitome of human activity, which allows "us to use creativity and imagination to see beyond the given and to search for missing information, physical reasons, and human purposes that will complete and explain the given" (p. 54).

However, creating an atmosphere for questioning and inquiry in a typical high school, where each teacher sees approximately 100–150 students per day, 25 or so at a time for less than an hour, is asking the impossible. It would require development of an infrastructure and processes that allow for personalizing education. For the purposes of clarifying our concept of learning, let it suffice to say that without allowance of questioning and inquiry on subjects and events that are important to the questioner at the time, real learning (of the cerebral cortex kind; i.e., problem-solving, critical thinking, creativity) cannot occur.

A questioning pedagogy, one that allows the person on the journey to question the why and wherefore of the elements encountered while upon the journey, is what learning is about. Meaningful learning engages the emotional, the feelings; it is just-in-time, authentic, and transformative, in that the learner wants to know now about something of importance *at the point at which they presently are in their journey!* Engaging the whole person in authentic experiences allows for a young person to not only *know* and *do*, but to *be* someone.

Tony Wagner, in his new book *Making the Grade: Reinventing America's Schools* (2001) refers to work of Daniel Golman on emotional intelligence. Golman says there is an emotional quotient that is as powerful, if not more powerful, than an intelligence quotient. These emotional intelligences include things like self-awareness, self-regulation, motivation, empathy and social skills. There appears to be no correlation between intelligence quotient and emotional quotient. The most important thing is that the emotional skills are more important in today's work-place than knowledge of information, because information is so vast and changes so quickly. Real learning is in this realm of *being*, or disposi-tions, or emotional quotient. And, as Wagner says, ". . . we do not yet know how to educate all students to these higher standards, nor do we know how to teach all students how to use new technologies. We've never had to do it before" (p. 17).

Extending consciousness, which could be said to be acquiring a *felt meaning* (Caine & Caine, 1994) is the act of becoming. *Knowing* is having facts, skills, and conceptual understandings we have acquired as a result of *doing* in the past. Taking action right now, in the present, with the knowledge, skills, and conceptions, is doing, and is the most important time because it is the present we live in. The chapter was be-gun with a quote taken from Gardner's discussion about understanding. It is about the *doing* processes. Learning could be seen as doing sets of performances, such as analysis, judgements, synthesis, and creating. These are what the New Country School emphasizes. But these processes should not be considered the final product, either.

Becoming is future oriented, looking forward to the next event and the possibilities it represents, then doing something about it now. Be-ing is more important than doing. Being is about developing disposi-tions that allow for higher order doing and creating future possibilities. Young learners are all about possibilities.

Meaningful learning, then, is having a sense of the *dispositions* and *competencies* young people need to create for themselves in their jour-ney that will allow them to create a life of possibilities. "The knowledge that matters most today *is not academic subject content. Competency— what we can do with knowledge—matters more than coverage*" (Wag-ner, 2001, p. 44). Meaningful learning, ultimately, leads to a learner ac-quiring skills to *become* a new person, a person that constantly reinvents him or herself. Acquiring the skills and dispositions to become "all that you can be" is what transformational education is about.

Know, Do, Be are not hierarchical taxonomies. A child can learn to know something by doing first. Certain dispositions, or ways of being, are necessary before doing and knowing. In many cases it requires knowing in order to do and then to be. But let us not lose sight of what the journey is about—*becoming*, fulfilling our full potential as humans, which ultimately requires dispositions and creative abilities. Just knowing is not good enough. Doing is more powerful, but should always be looked upon as unfinished. Being, in the now, and becoming, in the future, are what learning is about. When a learner can show others that they are acquiring dispositions that allow for them to create and recreate themselves in their connection to the world (and beyond, perhaps), then we can say learning is taking place.

CHAPTER 3

What Should We Assess and How Shall We Assess It?

> They know enough who know how to learn.
>
> —Henry Adams

In the last chapter we looked at the meaning of the word *learning* in order to establish what a meaningful learning experience really was. Having established that meaningful learning is acquiring dispositions and competencies that allow young people to become purposeful adults, we now turn to an explanation of how we know they are on the right path. In education we use two words, often without much distinction, to describe the process of "judging" where children are on their path to adulthood—evaluation and assessment. Consulting Webster's dictionary again, we find that *evaluate* means "to find or determine the amount, worth of." Do we really want to evaluate the attempt of children to acquire dispositions needed for adulthood? It hardly seems egalitarian to do so. Perhaps the children themselves may evaluate what they are seeking and finding, but for adults to place a value (such as an A, a B, or a C, etc.) on it appears rather arbitrary.

The word *assess* has an equally odious meaning, perhaps, as it means to evaluate for tax purposes. But, if we look at the root of the word, we find that the word assess comes from the Latin *assidere*, meaning to sit by, as a judge may sit by and determine what a person owns. This makes the term more palatable if we also take into account the pedagogue leading the novice along a path, occasionally sitting down with them to assess where they are on that journey. And, if we attach the concept that acquiring knowledge, skills and dispositions while along the path is the reason for the journey, what we have is a complete picture of meaningful learning, teaching, and assessing.

The dispositions and skills needed to negotiate a successful and meaningful life can be summed up in the SCANS skills mentioned in chapter 1: the ability to identify, organize, plan, and allocate resources; the ability to work with others; the ability to acquire and use information; the ability to understand complex interrelationships; and the ability to work with a variety of technologies. Or, the skills noted by professional pedagogues mentioned in chapter 2: good communication skills, mathematical abilities, a scientific understanding of the world, an understanding of how human beings interact; how to care for self and environment; and possibly, skills in and appreciation for the arts.

The important thing is to remember that the skills and dispositions needed for a successful life are at the forefront of what is assessed. The assessing and evaluating of bits and pieces of knowledge that are doled out in brief lessons is meaningless if the process cannot be seen in light of the larger picture. Certainly learners ought to know the facts. Certainly learners ought to be able to do certain skills. Certainly learners ought to understand processes and concepts. They do so, however, for the reason of attaining dispositions that they can carry with them throughout the rest of their lives. *People learn what they need to learn when they perceive the need to learn it!* This applies so very much to the concept of extending consciousness and developing dispositions. The facts, data, process, and conceptual framework of a discipline will be learned in the context of an authentic project because there is an interesting topic, a real world audience, and the project is carried on in the context of reality. Therefore, it is not so much an assessment of the facts and data (although that takes place), but the assessment of what dispositions were developed or enhanced by the learner using the correct facts, data, and processes.

Designs of assessment should be created by planning backward. We look first at the dispositions we want people to have, then the concepts and understandings needed to support them, then at the processes and skills needed to develop them, then at the facts and data that support the skills and processes. Each is assessed, but the end result that gets reported to the learner and other stakeholders are the concepts, skills, and dispositions, as they are the only things that will be leaving with the learner (no one retains all the facts they encountered in high school). This is called planning backward because planning what to assess is done not on what facts and data a student should know. Rather, that comes only after the concepts, processes, skills, and dispositions have been determined.

As mentioned in chapter 1, the project-based system changes the emphasis of assessment from short-term goals of facts, terms, and content to understanding complex ideas and processes: from mastery of isolated skills to mastery of integrated skills. Long-term goals change from breadth of knowledge to depth of knowledge: from performing successfully on standard achievement tests to acquiring dispositions and skills to engage in sustained, lifelong learning. Therefore, what we assess must be the complex ideas and processes, mastery of integrated skills, depth of knowledge, and the dispositions that allow for sustainable lifelong learning.

Every school should complete a mission statement. That mission statement should outline the major long-term goals for students who matriculate at that school. Assessment ought to come from the long-term goals articulated in that mission statement. Too often mission statements have become exercises in writing arcane poetry more so than workable documents. If you cannot assess the mission, then you do not have a mission.

In the project-based system created by the Minnesota New Country School, assessment has come to mean sitting by and judging where the student is in acquiring knowledge, concepts, skills and habits, or dispositions. By a process of internally applying action research, through trial and error, through applying external staff development opportunities, the staff at New Country settled on helping young people develop eight dispositions. These were developed from the work of Bill Spady (*Beyond Counterfeit Reforms*, 2000) in a workshop in 2001. The dispositions are life performance skills deemed by the staff as necessary in order to create a life of possibilities for the learner. They are:

- Leader & Organizer: being a person that others will follow, has a vision, gets things done, effectively uses time, does effective prioritizing, follows through, knows how to delegate.

- Mediator & Negotiator: being a person who is sought out for help, can resolve a problem, articulates sides and issues in a possible solution, demonstrates respect for various viewpoints, an open-minded, active listener.
- Coach & Facilitator: being a person who assists others in meeting goals, sticks to goals set for self, encourages others, works well with a team and with adults.
- Advocate & Supporter: being a person who will make a stand publicly, handles confidential information wisely, can back up opinions, and is "other centered."
- Implementer & Performer: being a person who has a positive effect on an audience, demonstrates high achievement and effectiveness in presentation, able to accept and apply constructive criticism, and creates a relationship with the community.
- Problem Framer/Solver: being a person who demonstrates the ability to use knowledge and skills to frame and solve complex, real-life problems, and can create projects that meet standards.
- Innovator & Designer: being a person who can create or invent new and unique solutions and/or products, a person willing to take risks even if they fail.
- Producer & Contributor: being a person who has the ability to create quality products, using correct information, with few blemishes, and one who consistently makes positive contributions to the community and the school.

These dispositional attributes are held up as the ideal to the students, are looked at and considered with every project when the staff "sits with" the student to assess the project, and are revisited whenever there is a parent-student conference.

It is worthwhile to point out that the first four listed are what is termed by Spady and others as the "emotional quotient," or EQ. The latter four are dispositions that represent the "intelligence quotient," or IQ. It is as important to help develop the emotional quotient of a person as it is the intelligence quotient. Too often the only things that get assessed in the traditional school system with the traditional teaching-learning system are the intelligence factors: often only at a lower level than dispositions (i.e., facts and figures, or declarative knowledge).

The difficulty we have with assessing the so-called soft skills, or dispositions and competencies, is that there are so many different actions that may or may not qualify to meet these new standards. Human beings are very complex, and adolescents even more so. What behaviors must be exhibited in order to say that a learner is actually developing the skill of being a leader? Or an organizer?

The pedagogues of the Minnesota New Country School have struggled with that, and still do. In their journey of the past seven years, the advisors have used a variety of means to understand what skills learners are actually developing, and what are behaviors that show that. At first, the connection between what learners do in project development, and what they produce as outcomes, were considered.

In the development of projects, due to the nature of adolescents and human nature in general, learners had to know that time was precious. The first major problem project-based models incur is the reluctance of teens to utilize time toward an objective. So, time journals and logs were added, and the project rubric included two different time-oriented tasks: documentation of time and effort, and task completion. The first required students to document in journals or logs how they used their time in that particular project. These logs or journals had to be handed in with the project, and were assessed as part of the total picture. The second had to do with timelines established in the project proposal, and how well they were met. This, too, was considered as part of the overall assessment.

How does this relate to learning? If learning is dispositional, it has a great deal to do with it. The habit of using time wisely is an excellent disposition and fits into the rubric as organizer, producer, and problem framer/solver. Learners need to know that, need to practice that, and have it become second nature. It is also important for management of the overall learning environment, and learners ought to know that. When large numbers of adolescents are brought together in a small space, time management becomes paramount.

Also, having time management as a major portion of the assessment allows for learners to self-regulate and self-assess. Having time documentation and task completion as important elements tells students that they need to keep track of what they do, why they do what they do, and with whom they do it. Of course, articulation of why they need to do it is also critical. If learners know that these time-oriented tasks are there to help them develop self-awareness, self-assessment, and self-management, and they are there to help them become better organizers, producers, and problem-solvers, then you ought to have more intrinsically motivated learners. This articulation is why the mission statement and goals of the school being implemented and articulated are so vitally critical to every aspect of the model being successful: from students being more purposeful to marketing the school to parents.

Other dispositional aspects of the assessment rubrics used by the New Country staff include project assessment by the learner. Self-assessment of what a student is doing, having the student create their own assessment structure for that particular project, gives a sense of ownership and helps develop the self-awareness, self-regulation elements of organizer, producer, problem-solver, implementer, and performer. Similarly, having the student be aware of their ownership of the project (that is, their understanding that they must create a model, product, process or idea that is unique) is a powerful way to have students become more self-aware, self-regulatory, and leads to the dispositional competency of being an innovator and designer. Project quality is considered so learners see the need to self-regulate and self-assess in producing, implementing, designing, and contributing. Being aware of a variety of resources and showing means by which those various types of resources are used, is another basic competency that leads to being an organizer, problem framer/solver, implementer, producer, and contributor. Without having the knowledge base, without making a good case for what your project product is about, the student would not show the dispositions necessary to be a purposeful adult.

Another element of the assessment rubrics designed by the New Country staff is the critical thinking piece. Because it is not enough to simply have a series of disconnected facts produced, not enough just to regurgitate facts found and developed by someone else, but rather it is necessary to use knowledge meaningfully, learners needed to know the difference. The rubric also includes three elements developed by Robert Marzano (1993) in his work on the Dimensions of Learning. First, the project assessors check to see if the learner comprehends the facts gathered. In other words, did they just write out someone else's words and thoughts, or did they put thoughts in their own words and use them for their own purposes? And did the learner successfully attend to new knowledge in that arena or discipline; did they find enough useful information to adequately explain the concept they are trying to describe?

Secondly, did the learner utilize the knowledge to exhibit retention (could they explain the process or concept in their own words) and could they exhibit how they used the knowledge to contribute their own "take" on the situation or concept? Thirdly, did the learner use the information in multiple real contexts, as the knowledge or process would be used in the real world? If so, the product or performance would have an authenticity, would actually be useful to the adult world, and not just be something the student had to do to get credits.

If the learner obtained relatively high marks on those critical thinking skills, they again exhibit abilities as organizers, advocates, implementers, designers, problem framers/solvers, producers, and contributors. Remember, as pointed out earlier in this chapter, what we assess must be the complex ideas and processes, mastery of integrated skills, depth of knowledge, and the dispositions that allow for sustainable life-long learning. Assessment of the dispositions that account for *being* and *doing*, rather than simply for *knowing* gives the school the overall culture of a purposeful place that values the journey to adulthood.

An element that has not been addressed as of yet, and is very critical in these times of high standards, is how the project-based model addresses and assesses the state standards. In Minnesota, the state education department (the Department of Children, Families and Learning) had developed over the past nine years what is called the Profiles of Learning. The Profiles are organized around ten areas or disciplines (although the state curriculum is designed to be integrative, it is still organized around the major disciplines). The Profiles are inquiry based, allowing for the integration of subject matter along some of the disciplines. Therefore, the Profiles of Learning make a project-based system viable by stressing inquiry, process, and integration.

State standards that are tied to traditional disciplines and are content oriented become much more difficult to meet in the project-based system. Before implementing the project-based system, it would be necessary to obtain a waiver of content-oriented standards or to look at content-oriented standards in a more general way. In other words, content in itself should only help explain general concepts and inter-connectedness, not separation and fragmentation. If content is not leading to a connectedness, meaning a sense of how all disciplines are integrated and how the real world works, then it is doing a disservice rather than a service. Looking at content standards in a general and integrated way is better for overall understanding, and leads to dispositional *being* rather than simply *knowing*.

How a school curriculum team can take content standards and develop integrated project-based learning around them is a major challenge. It can be done, but requires more ingenuity and work. What must be understood is that content is always involved with projects—just not in the way schools usually organize content. So the attempt must be made to utilize as much of the content as possible, but not to let it get in the way of learning *doing* and *being* skills. And if people criticize the fact that you are not implementing all the content standards, ask them how much content is retained and used by traditional students? Or, better yet, ask those criticizing how many of those content standards, outside of their specific field, do they know?

When the subject of content versus process comes up, just ask people what it is that is important to know to become a productive adult. No one can agree on what content that would take, anyway. Most people whose livelihood depends on the teaching of a certain set of discipline standards would in all likelihood name theirs as most important. This phenomenon is exactly why we have over 3,500 content standards in some state curriculums.

According to research done by Tony Wagner of Harvard University, parents, teachers and the general public all believe basic skills in reading, writing, and mathematics are the most important reason for schooling. Basic skills, for the most part, are considered to be at the tenth-grade level at best. So where are the other content areas in the list of most important skills for high school students to have? Of the top eight items in the survey, only American History and geography are listed as high priority.

The second most important skill on all lists was good work habits, such as being responsible, on time, and disciplined. Perhaps the traditional system does a good job in this department, but rarely assesses it as such. The third most important skill, according to the poll, was *us-*

age of computer skills and media technology. How much usage of technology takes place in traditional school, if the students have to be in classes of various disciplines all day?

The fourth major skill was the value of hard work. Again, the traditional system can claim to do something here, but usually only in context of what work students put into earning grades in disciplines. Rarely is the disposition of "hard working" in itself an assessable item. Fifth on the list was the value of honesty and tolerance of others. This disposition is one the traditional system does have trouble with—when content is king, cheating is easier. Tidbits of knowledge are easy to obtain just before a test. Dispositions must be shown over long periods of time.

The sixth most important attribute according to the poll was acquiring habits of good citizenship, such as voting and caring for the nation. Again, I would say that memorizing the civics text is not going to get this done. Learners need to be *doing* citizenship, learning the facts and vocabulary as they go along, rather than memorizing. A project-based system allows for the doing, therefore the becoming. The next skill is knowing how to deal with social problems. Facts and figures in this arena change, but dispositions do not.

One area that the parents and public differed widely from teachers was the knowledge of American History and geography. Eighty-three percent of teachers said this was important, placing it fifth on their list. It was eighth on the list of parents and the general public. Knowledge of these arenas is important. I am a history and geography teacher myself. But I learned that acquiring facts (for a short time) and retaining them (for a long time) are entirely two different things. Learners may acquire and retain some highly selective facts in order to pass tests. But they certainly are not going to retain them all. So, how can the most important concepts be retained so that they can be used over and over again? And what are those most important concepts?

Ninth on the list was curiosity and love of learning. Sixty-nine percent of teachers listed this as important, as opposed to 61% and 57% of the parents and public. I would have listed this as my most important, as it makes the others possible. It is what the project-based system is about, and makes it possible for learners to acquire the other dispositions and skills necessary to go about learning *what they need to learn when they perceive the need to learn it.*

The point is, generally speaking, the public knows that knowledge is of less importance than dispositions. Concepts are more important to understand than tidbits of knowledge. In other words, as Marzano (1993) has instructed us, using knowledge to create deeper understandings and habits of mind is more important than being able to regurgitate facts on tests. Or, as put by Caine & Caine (1994), an inner appreciation of interconnectedness, felt meaning for the whole, is the root of reflective intelligence. From the *doing* comes the *being*. From *doing* and *being* can come *knowing*. It isn't always that we have to know first in order to do—sometimes doing leads to knowing. The traditional system often believes that the dispositions (such as hard work, honesty, good work habits) should be part of a students life before they come to school, so why not believe in doing before knowing?

In any event, the process of doing projects can and does, in the case of the system devised by the Minnesota New Country School, link state inquiry standards with dispositions. Basic skills are measured by state-mandated tests—all students must pass tests on reading, writing, and math before they can graduate. These are met by personalizing the projects so that learners needing extra help in attaining the basic skills will have the resources, tutoring, time, and help they need.

The school helps students meet the high standards, the Profiles of Learning, by first making the standards known to the student. Each student gets a Curriculum Standards Guidebook with the state standards stated in their general form, each general standard with a check blank before them. When a student completes a standard, the blank is checked. The student continues to meet standards, most often different ones from different disciplines, from the same project. Or, they can meet a standard specifically by doing a series of "assignments" and producing a number of products that prove to the teacher/advisors that the standard is met. Students are expected to meet 24 high standards, of a possible 30 available.

Because the learner has the curriculum standards guidebook, they become very familiar, in time, with what the standards mean. It is often the case that the students can explain a standard better than a teacher can, especially if it is out of the teacher's general area of expertise. That, however, comes only after the advisor and learner work at it for some time. The job of advisor from the very first is to help the learner to understand what the standards mean and what it would take to meet them. This often takes a collective effort, as advisors advise learners in all standards; therefore, they must consult other advisors with other licenses and expertise. It is common for New Country students to visit with a number of advisors, not only their own, and with a variety of resources to discover the full meaning of standards and what it would take to meet them.

At first learners "attack" the standards via an interest in a topic, and between them and the advisor brainstorm what standards may be met by doing so. For example, if the learner has an interest in horses, it is the task of the advisor to make the learner aware of the number of possible areas such a project may meet. The learner could show their ability to read complex information, scientific reading, or interpreting perspectives. In writing, they could either write a technical manual on the care and raising of horses, or an academic piece on the history of the horse in North America. The learner could also develop a public speech and give that speech at a Presentation Night. (Each learner has to present three of their projects to the public. In those presentations, the learners are expected to show they have developed presentation skills, knowledge and application of the topic, organization and problem solving, and have shown a well-designed display or product.)

Mathematics may be more difficult to engage, but it is possible to create some problems showing the learner's skill in patterns and discrete functions, chance and data handling, measurement, or shape and space. The advisor and learner need to be creative and work from the standards back to the possibilities in the research.

The Horse Project could also incorporate history through culture, cultures across time, cultural interaction with environment, and themes of U.S. history. The project could be about the anatomy of the horse, the genetics of horse raising, and about nutrition for horses, thereby incorporating a biological element. And, if the learner was particularly ambitious, they could research and create a business plan around creating a horse ranch. This would also allow for the learner to incorporate career investigation into the mix.

Very rarely would a project incorporate all of the above. The learner would want to finish a project before the year was over. But, it does offer insight into the multiple opportunities that await the learner and the enterprising advisor. Be aware that each of the general areas of standards mentioned are also broken down into smaller units, and in many cases only parts of standards would be met. Other parts would have to be met with subsequent projects. By using this process, however, if a learner applied him or herself, 24 of the 30 possible standards could be met in a four-year span.

The evaluation of each project has to include the assessment of information used in order to know if the standard is met. The learner cannot produce a product (such as a business plan for developing a horse ranch) without having real facts and figures. They cannot write about the horse in Dakota history without having the facts. They cannot create a video or PowerPoint presentation about horse breeding if they don't have the facts right and cannot operate the computer program. It is the job of advisors to either know the right facts, or to find sources that do have them.

One of the unique methods employed by the New Country staff is the requirement of learners to have outside human sources for their projects. The learner must contact experts in the field to obtain information or to learn about good, up-to-date sources of information. Also, the method of assessment, utilizing two advisors and one outside person, usually assures that the standards of knowledge and quality of product is up to standard. The parents also have the opportunity to sign off on the project, getting their input as well (more about the process in chapter 6).

When the project is finished (and it is not finished until it is worthy of being called finished), the assessment team "sits by" the learner to quiz and question them on the information (*knowing*), the process and presentation (*doing*), and also assesses the dispositional skills displayed (*being*). It is possible that learners may not have all the facts to make a case or prove a point or meet a standard. If so, they are asked to correct the mistake and review their product, presentation, etc., then resubmit. This iterative process makes it likely that success will eventually be achieved, if time does not become the major factor. Also, as a rubric is used, a learner may not make a high score in all areas in order to get credit for a project, but must show progress in that area over time. That means that some standards may be met with a completed project, and others may not. Therefore a learner may have to "attack" that standard again another time.

The unique method of incorporating state standards into projects and assessing them in all three types of learning make the New Country system of project-based learning a viable model for others to follow. It is the power of the system, and it is what helps maintain the construct for developing and maintaining a passion for learning. When teachers create curriculum around their perceived needs, when they try to incorporate the public and professional pedagogue's standards into those perceived needs to complicate them, they also create a hostile environment for students. Students and parents often feel left out of curriculum and assessment. The Minnesota New Country School process allows for the passion of the learner and the common sense of the parent to be employed in the learning process.

CHAPTER 4

What Is the Role of the Teacher?

The art of teaching is the art of assisting discovery.

—Mark Van Doren

The pedagogue who assists the child upon their journey toward adulthood has a very important part to play. Part parent, part philosopher, part guru, part friend, part antagonist, part magician, a teacher must be many things to many people. In the world of the project-based school this role expands even further. Being in the role of advisor (as our project-based schools call the teachers) is a demanding job. Teaching in any type of school is a demanding job. What is at the heart of good teaching, regardless of what type of teaching you do?

Parker Palmer in his wonderful book *The Courage to Teach*, says the most commonly asked question is the "what" question, followed by the "how" question, followed by the "why" question. These are all well and good, but a more important question has to be asked—the "who" question. A teacher/advisor has to think in terms of what it is he/she brings to the table prior to being prepared to work with children in an educational institution. What is brought to the learner ought to be a person who is intellectually, emotionally, and spiritually grounded. Only a person who knows who they really are in a holistic sense, one who has been transformed into a purposeful adult, can truly bring about such a transformation in others.

When teaching a methods class to pre-service teachers, I always alluded to the three Cs needed to be a good teacher. Those were caring, competence, and confidence. I since have amended the three Cs to the *five* Cs, the first being *centeredness*. By this I mean having a great sense of selfhood, at peace intellectually, emotionally, and spiritually. If there is doubt in any area, it will come through in interactions with learners and coworkers. A centered person knows where they are in the great scheme of the universe, who they are in relation to all others, what they are about, and has a sense of purpose. How does this happen? From a good upbringing, having a good family support system, knowing that they are loved, and having a feeling of self-efficacy. The backgrounds may be quite different. It has always amazed me to see the variations of types of individual personalities that make effective teachers. Tall, short, kind, tough, type As, type Bs, single, married, it hardly matters. What does matter is that the person who teaches is at peace with himself or herself, that they accept who they are, and know that they *matter* to the world.

From this centeredness can come *caring*. Only when a person has a strong sense of self can they truly care about others. They must care about others if they wish to be teacher/advisors. To be the responsible guide on the side of the journeying adolescent toward responsible adulthood demands a large measure of kindness and a largess of heart. If there is not a real affinity for youth, a real sense of duty toward helping young people find themselves and their place in the world, it will be a task without reward and soon will evolve into drudgery and apathy.

Adolescent learners will know whether or not you care about them or whether it is just another job for you. And caring is not simply being a kind, grandmotherly person. Anyone who has parented or taught teens knows they need "tough love" sometimes, understanding and comforting other times. But always, they need to be listened to and respected for who they are. Persons who care about who they are, and who went through being nurtured, who have felt unconditional love, can more honestly show love and respect for others.

When a teacher/advisor is centered and has an affinity (caring) for youth, the *competence* in what they teach will be more evident. In the first place, a centered individual knows he/she is capable, is self-efficacious. Learning, in whatever domain or discipline, should be a joyous and fulfilling task. If it is not, then don't be a teacher. It is necessary to bring that joy to the school environment and to express it to the learners. When a teacher/advisor is competent and shows enjoyment in learning and explaining, then learners will catch a spirit of enjoyment from them. A centered, caring, and competent person will move, touch, and inspire.

The fourth element is *confidence*. Nothing can erode a person's confidence faster than to have to listen to adolescents continually question who you are, what you are doing, and why you are there. If a person does not come into the teaching profession with a strong sense of confidence in who they are (centeredness) and in what they know (competence), and without a strong sense of caring about young people, there will be a lack of effectiveness. Confidence is, however, a trait that needs to build upon successful activities, as well as being an attribute brought to the task. Nothing can build confidence better than to have a strong sense of selfhood and knowing your "stuff." But you have to show them you care that you know what you are doing, and that you *believe* in what you are doing. Even though there will still be many days when the negativism appears overwhelming, staying strong will eventually win over most of those with whom you come into contact.

The fifth element is *creating*. Notice that I did not say creativity. That is part of it, but not all. Creating means you need to be continually re-creating yourself by being a life-long learner. A strong teacher/advisor is continually exhibiting the joy of learning new things, and bringing what they know to the educational environment. Young people need guides who are still on the journey, and who have the wherewithal to expect to learn *with* the others on the pilgrimage to adulthood: because adulthood is not a destination, but a journey in and of itself. When young people see that a teacher/advisor can and does learn with them, sees that the leader is enthused and excited about learning new things, inspiration to discover will carry over.

After all, the art of teaching is the art of assisting discovery: discovery of self, how to relate to others, how the world is made up and how it works. Teacher/advisors are not merely to be "givers of information" about how the world works, but need to be the proverbial "guide on the side" for a learner to discover the world in the true constructivist sense.

With that in mind, it is necessary to look at what an advisor ought to be able to do in order to facilitate the project-based learning system. Teachers, in order to understand and utilize the project-based model, need to develop a mind-set and instructional methodologies that transcend the traditional orientations toward teaching. Caine & Caine (1997), in the book *Unleashing the Power of Perceptual Change*, consider that teachers generally are taught one orientation (that of the stand-and-deliver) and that the standard educational establishments support that orientation. In the past two decades, educational psychologists and brain researchers have developed the constructivist theory, which cannot be fully utilized by using the typical and standard orientation methodology. To fully support the personalized, project-based, and integrated education method, the teacher mind-set must reflect new orientations toward learning and teaching. Also, a set of expectations and skills needed for teaching in these types of schools is necessary.

First, according to Caine & Caine, a teacher must *make the transition from power over others to self-efficacy grounded in authenticity* (p. 91), what I would consider part of centeredness. Advisors in project-based schools must see that power and decision making rests in themselves and in the learner, and not in others. In order to do this, they must have a solid sense of identity, and believe they can affect change in themselves, in students, and in the system. A self-efficacious advisor is a creative teacher, one not afraid to delve into the unknown and create some new relationships, new activities, and new ways of doing things.

Although creative, the advisor must also have their actions grounded in authenticity, in the "real world." A teacher in these model schools is comfortable with where they have come from, where they are, and where they can help take the learner. Knowing how the "real" world works is essential, and knowing how to tie academic material to authentic uses is important.

An authentic advisor can also handle self-disclosure, because they are authentic and real. The ideal pedagogue/leader will not be afraid of being known, therefore interacting with the public, parents, and others in the school. There should be no hiding behind the "ivory tower" door. An authentic, empowered, self-efficacious leader will undertake to lead learners, work with other advisors, communicate with parents, and be a community leader as well.

A teacher is a facilitator/advisor, not a deliverer of knowledge. Hence, they are able to allow for the student to take over their own learning. If they truly believe in being a facilitator of knowledge acquisition, then they actually will facilitate and advise, not deliver.

A project-based advisor should also have *expanded cognitive horizons* (p. 115), and be able to see the big picture; that the world is the curriculum and that the world's knowledge on the application level is entirely integrated. They can deal with complex content and not feel the need to hold on to the preeminence of their own field of expertise.

The advisor also understands the difference between facts, concepts, and levels of meaning. The advisor also knows that there are many dimensions to learning; that declarative or factual knowledge is not an end in itself; that applying, refining, and extending knowledge are skills necessary for high school level students; and that developing dispositional skills is more important than factual knowledge.

Although having a cosmopolitan sense about knowledge, the advisor will have expertise in at least one discipline and have a "felt meaning" for other disciplines (Caine & Caine, 1997). They should have a sense of wholeness and interconnectedness, allowing them to see connections between disciplines and life in general. It is imperative that the facilitator/advisor sees that process is as important or more important than mere knowledge of facts.

A project-based, constructivist advisor *will have a sense of self-reference and process* (p. 131). They will possess reflective intelligence and understand mindfulness. If advisors are capable of understanding how they themselves learn, they may then help learners build their own metacognitive skills. By observing, understanding, and questioning themselves and the world around them, they know how to turn a question around so students can find their own answer. They can use the "questioning pedagogy" mentioned earlier, and not always demand the "right" answer.

The guiding pedagogue also should *move from control to building relationships that facilitate self-organization* (p. 150). The advisor will understand the relationship between information and experience and understand the relationship between learning and context. And because they are not the deliverer of knowledge, but the facilitator of students becoming self-taught, they can understand that the relationship between students and teachers is one of mentor to novice rather than one of authority figure to antagonist. A facilitator will know the importance of self-regulation, and will work with students to establish orderly processes, routines, and procedures. Discipline is a secondary concern because learning is organized around meaningful projects and activities. They allow students to take responsibilities and keep their own sense of order, help others assess where learners are on their journey, and allow students to challenge each other.

Caine & Caine (1997) refer to teachers' having one or more of three orientations. They simply call them orientation one, two, and three. The orientation-one teacher is a direct-instruction teacher, with the orientation-three teacher being a facilitator of learning. Following are differences between the orientations in a number of education behaviors:

For the orientation-one teacher, the object of instruction is to have the learner acquire surface knowledge, with small, incremental outcomes. The learner is to acquire facts, skills, and information through memorization, practice, and repetition using taxon memory. The educational system artificially imposes times, usually 50–55 minute periods. Deadlines are imposed by the teacher via lesson plans and unit plans. Generally they cannot abide the student's need of extra time. The sources of curriculum and instruction are designated guides, books, and what students "should" know. The teacher-selected instruction is by lecture, reading of texts, paper-pencil assignments, and demonstrations on designated subjects and topics. Generally the orientation-one teacher's approach to discipline is authoritative. The teacher governs behavior, controls disruptions, writes rules, and reviews punishments. The emphasis is on behaviorism and "assertive discipline."

The orientation-one teacher's basis of assessment is on replication of teacher and source material, paper-pencil tests, quizzes, often with true-false and multiple choice tests, always with a right and wrong answer. The educational setting is usually stand-and-deliver, with the teacher part of larger system with curricular expectations dominated by *transmission* of knowledge. Grades are a means of control, hours are negotiated; the system dominates, not the individual needs of the learners

In orientation two, the object of instruction is highly focused on behavioral outcomes, with the learner's purpose still secondary. Learners are to acquire scholastic knowledge, with an understanding of ideas and concepts through teacher-led activities. The teacher orchestrates and controls activities, still uses 50–55 minute periods, lesson plans and unit plans, but uses some thematic and integrative activities. The sources of curriculum and instruction are instructional source books, curriculum guides, some primary sources, and the state curriculum. The teacher uses planned activities, highly structured thematic instruction, and exploration.

The orientation-two teacher's approach to discipline is one of listening and communicating in a structured setting, while creating community in the classes. Failure to cooperate is a disruption. Some constructivist activities are allowed.

The orientation-two teacher assesses by developing group and individual problem-solving activities and projects, and establishes some structured performance rubrics. The teacher still controls assessment and evaluation, and will still use paper-pencil tests on occasion. The educational setting is made up of more thematic activities and cooperative learning. Hands-on activities are used if they fit the time frames. The emphasis is on teacher strategies and instructions that can be creative and move beyond packaged materials. Emphasis is on the *transaction* of knowledge and skills.

The facilitator/advisor in orientation three has as the object of instruction learning-to-learn skills, the acquisition of critical thinking, and problem-solving skills. They strive for integration of subject matter, with holistic real-world outcomes. The advisor uses an inquiry-based methodology. The advisor uses time to present problems, helps the learner to make sense of their problems, works with individuals and groups establishing student responsibilities; therefore time is flexible and fluid.

The sources of curriculum and instruction are real-world actions. Projects are created around student interests and needs, with parents and community experts playing a part. Real-world situations, the advisor's experiences, and student experiences are used to create projects. It is as close to a pure constructivist methodology as possible. The approach to discipline is one of low threat and high challenge. The goal is "relaxed alertness" (Caine & Caine, 1994), with learner development of intrinsic motivation desired. The project process sets goals and therefore helps with time management.

The advisor assesses using performance rubrics, time management rubrics, project-process checklists, state inquiry standards, and life performance rubrics. The educational setting is one where learners lead activities, with unstructured time demanding open structures. Time is flexible, fluid, and open-ended. There would be student workstations and advisor-advisee groups with a multiage structure. The emphasis is on a *transformational* education

In order to be a facilitator of skill acquisition, therefore an *advisor* rather than a *teacher*, requires the pedagogue to be willing to let go of the direct instruction model of orientation one. If a teacher has never moved into orientation two, they will probably never be able to move to orientation three. Many good teachers have attempted to develop the orientation-two methods and found the system of strictly controlled time and management of curriculum in their way. The practitioners at the New Country School and other replication sites found that you have to be willing to allow for a more flexible system, yet with structure enough to give learners a path to follow. What we as educators believe becomes the primary driver of how we think about the education setting. If you truly believe the constructivist philosophy, then it may be necessary to change the setting entirely.

One of the barriers to doing so, and one that is necessary to overcome, is what I call the *peculiar conceit*. It appears as if all teachers (and I include myself as a young teacher) have the idea that learners must know all of the factual knowledge within the particular discipline they teach. Or, at least a major portion thereof. Orientation-one teachers feel they cannot offer up time for projects and hands-on activities because they have to "cover" so much material, as if all the learners are going to remember it anyway. The conceit in this is twofold: that students will remember everything you cover, and that they actually need to know it. In twenty or more years of teaching, I have witnessed a number of students who did poorly in my history classes do quite well as citizens. Who was I to assume they would be poor citizens because they did not have a passion for what I had a passion for?

I wish I had a dollar for every time I heard a teacher say something like: "I don't know anything about math; I can only teach what I know." Or, "It's not my job to teach writing, and I'm not qualified, anyway." Listening closely to those comments one has to determine that teachers don't know facts and skills from other teachers' disciplines. How did they get out of high school, anyway? Let alone college?

Of course we don't remember everything from our high school classes. It is an impertinence to make that assumption. We know well what we teach, but to assume that high school learners must know as much as we do about our subjects is indeed a peculiar conceit. Are facts and skills important? Are concepts in science and math important to understand? Of course, but we must be willing as teachers to come down off our high horses and make a fundamental determination of what truly important facts and skills are necessary to be a productive adult. We need to give up some of our "coverage," and allow that to be productive a learner needs to know *how to learn* and will *want to learn*. If they are turned off by the rigid rules, the rigid curriculum, and don't get to practice being adult-like in their behavior, then we have done them a disservice. The true art of teaching is the art of assisting discovery, not disseminating information.

Assuming a teacher is willing to become an advisor and facilitator of learning, is willing to adopt orientation-three beliefs and methods, then it is possible to be a project-based learning advisor. But to truly be an effective advisor, there are many skills necessary. One, as already alluded to, is to be a generalist first, an expert second. When facilitating learner-centered projects, you must be able to see that larger cognitive picture mentioned before, be flexible, self-reflective, and be willing to build relationships rather than control learner behavior at all times.

A teacher who is willing to become an advisor needs to understand that new skills will be expected of them. Instead of the standard skills (that of deliverer of curriculum, classroom discipline, and dutiful employee), the facilitator/advisor of a teacher-owned school will need to exhibit the following skills. The highest level of achievement on the staff skill rubric designed by New Country School staff is mentioned in order to show what an exemplary advisor is capable of, and should aspire to become.

In the area of advisor/learner relationships, the advisor will establish excellent rapport, show great caring of the learners in their care, and take great interest in their lives outside of school. The advisor will establish and maintain consistent standards of behavior, make the environment safe and conducive to learning in the project-based methodology.

The advisor will challenge all students to do their best, encourage them to extend and refine their thinking, encourage students to fulfill the state standards, and give excellent feedback to all students. The advisor will have knowledge of how to create and select exemplary instructional resources and materials for students and show a clear understanding of content standards necessary to be fulfilled.

In addition, the advisor will organize their actions and the student activities extremely well, use instructional time in an excellent fashion, and keep exemplary records of student activity. The advisor will understand and help the learner to make connections between content standards, create and select excellent assessment strategies, and make learning goals very clear to students.

In working with parents, the advisor will establish and maintain an excellent relationship, listen to parents and act upon the concerns of parents. The advisor will inform parents of student needs and advisor concerns, keep good records, and have excellent conferencing skills. The advisor will always be accessible for parent calls, and will take time to meet with parents when needed.

While working with staff, the advisor will build professional relationships, share teaching insights, and help coordinate learning activities for all learners. The advisor should be willing to give extra time and duties to the support of learners, staff, and to the school generally. The advisor will rarely take time off and when doing so makes leave accommodations with other staff members. The advisor should be willing to take on extra duties and roles, fulfill board and committee positions, and use extra time to engage the public with promotion of the school.

In addition, an advisor will be willing to develop their own personal growth as an educational reformer by being willing to do professional reading, take classes, and attend conferences to enhance their knowledge of progressive and constructivist education. The advisor will be willing to try what has been learned at professional gatherings or from readings, and often engage in conversation about new ideas with colleagues. The advisor should be willing and able to spend extra time to prepare and present material at state and national conferences to promote the school model. In addition, an advisor will develop an action research plan around a personal growth plan, student achievement, and new ideas.

It is also necessary to carry on good community relations, especially as a project-based school will more than likely, for a time, be unique in the community. The advisor should participate in community relationships, marketing, and promotion of the school, within both the smaller and larger community. The advisor will repeatedly establish community contacts to help in student projects.

In order to move from the regular orientation-one delivery-of-information method to the orientation-three facilitator-of-disposition-acquisition methods, the New Country founders adopted an advisor-advisee system of one advisor to approximately 17 students. As advisor of these 17, an educator would be responsible for keeping track of the progress along the life performance continuum adopted by the school. Also, an advisor would track the progress on the statewide curriculum and the number of project credits, time management rubrics, etc., the staff develops.

The primary work of an advisor would be to help each of these 17 students devise projects that meet various criteria out of the student's interests. This is where the *passion for learning* is developed, and is critical to the whole process. An advisor must know the student well. An independent learner plan should be created for each student via a three-way conference with parents, student, and advisor.

An excellent method for learning about the learner under advisement is to administer a psychological profile test of some sort. Avalon Charter School in St. Paul has begun using an assessment called the Motivational Appraisal of Personal Potential (MAPP), which determines worker traits such as: interest in job content, temperament for the job, aptitude for a job, how the learner relates to people, relates to things, relates to data, relates to reasoning procedures, mathematical capacity, and language capacity. It also measures the mental orientation, the perceptual orientation, how a learner relates to media, preferred learning environments, preferred classroom environments, and skills for testing procedures. From this psychological profile assessment, an advisor would have a very clear picture of what are the learners' capacities, interests, strengths, and weaknesses. I have tried this assessment myself and found it almost eerily accurate about my preferred work and learning styles. Having a sense of what work a learner may have an aptitude for is a motivating factor to create projects around the capabilities. It is an advantage to know where the weaknesses are, so frustrations surrounding accomplishing certain tasks are understood. The results of this survey should be used in the three-way conference to determine the goals for the learner.

When a learner's interests, strengths, and weaknesses are known, then a goal can be set for what projects to develop and what will help develop the passion for learning in that learner. Also, the advisor would help their students with developing projects around standards when the learner has come to the understanding they need to create projects around concepts and ideas that are not of their choosing, but are found in the state curriculum. The advisor is also responsible for the management of the learner's time.

An advisor interacts and works with other learners in the education setting by advising on their expertise or discipline area. Learners from other advisory groups would ask for an advisor with a science degree, for example, to help with a project that would have a chemistry component. Or an advisor would be on the assessment team for a student of another advisory group.

The task of being an advisor in this system is truly the art of assisting discovery. It is understood that teaching is not delivery of information, but the art of developing young learners' passions for and abilities to learn in the future as well as in the now. The dispositions and philosophy needed for advisors to carry out this task may not be a fit for every educator. But if the right educators can be found, the fulfillment of the orientation-three constructivist philosophy toward education, the assisting of young people on their journey toward a purposeful adulthood, is not only possible but probable.

Admittedly these skills for an advisor are quite encompassing and, perhaps, daunting. But for a pedagogue to be the kind of leader, mentor, and guide that learners need in order to become purposeful adults, it is necessary to be productive adults that aspire to all of the above beliefs and skills. And that is being a centered, caring, competent, confident, creating, orientation-three advisor, willing to build relationships with students, parents, and the community. It can be done. It is being done, as many of the advisors at the New Country School and other replication sites are showing daily.

CHAPTER 5

What Should the School Look Like?

The shoe that fits one person pinches another; there is no recipe for living that suits all cases.

—Carl Jung

The form of something often dictates the function for which it is used. The founders and practitioners at the New Country School, and the replication sites, have found that attempting to squeeze a project-based learning program into the regular comprehensive high school architectural format does, indeed, pinch toes. If a building has classrooms, they will be used as gathering places for "classes" of students to have information delivered to them by orientation-one teachers. In almost every school building in America (and beyond), the industrial model prevails. Even in the discussions on infrastructure needs for the twenty-first century, school leaders are calling for billions of dollars to rebuild dilapidated school buildings in the same form as they are now. Rarely is there talk of creating new sorts of environments, and where there is, there is some resistance or reticence. The old sorts of learning environments were created not with the goal in mind of student-centered learning, but the goal of teacher-centered delivery of "peculiar conceits."

In the 1970s a series of "open classroom" model schools were created. Too soon, however. Because so little was know then about the need for brain-based learning and constructivist methods, teachers and administrators had a difficult time using the open spaces, and soon they were pulled back into the traditional classroom model. This failure is used to justify the continual building of large, comprehensive high schools with the 1960s' mentality: large units with classrooms for each teacher, gymnasiums and athletic fields for the community (not always just for the students), cafeterias to handle hundreds, media centers, and computer labs in former classrooms. Architects can only play around with the looks and the materials—the design is practically the same everywhere.

This one-size-fits-all mentality does not allow for the research-supported personalized learning environments that would allow for learner-centered activities to occur. Learning is too highly personalized to fit into a model that is designed for mass-produced results. Where each learner needs to have a personalized learning plan, and space to actively create the outcomes, the old model of school does not fit.

In a project-based system, classrooms as the dominant feature of a building are not primary. Any building that offers open spaces that can be divided up into various workspaces for advisory groups will work. The basic components of space usage for a project-based, advisory group oriented school are:

One, to have an open space or area where each student can own a workstation of their own. For a student to have a workstation that belongs particularly to him or her is a powerful way to provide ownership in the school. The workstation becomes a home-away-from-home for the learner. They may decorate it (within reason) to give it a personal touch; they may have organizers, boxes, backpacks, even foodstuffs at their workstations if they so desire. The New Country School in Minnesota has made it a mission to provide almost every student with a computer at their workstation (as of this writing there is one computer for every 1.5 students in the school). If learners do not have computers at their workstation, computers in a media center or in other areas are usually available. When students have a place of their own, with the tools for resources (such as computers), they do not see the school as belonging to the principal or the school board. Nor do they see themselves going to Mr. Jones' room, or Mrs. Johnson's room; rather they see themselves coming into a place where they are welcomed and respected as individuals.

Two, space should be created for an advisory group to be housed. A space with 17–18 workstations and an advisor's desk, in one area, allow for a family atmosphere to exist. The advisory group lives with each other for a year (or longer). The advisor will get to know the learners in that group on a much more intimate scale than a typical high school teacher, who may see 150 students a day. Advisory groups usually are multiaged, with the possibility of 13 year olds housed with 18 year olds. This allows older learners to mentor younger learners. It allows for a more family-like existence. Often advisory groups will be developed back-to-back, with only some low dividers between them, similar to an office building. Movement between advisory groups may often occur, with students able to move relatively freely from one place to another.

A third necessity for a project-based program to thrive is having open, flexible space so that students may utilize it for a variety of uses. The open space could have tables and chairs available, so students may congregate at various times for various purposes. This open space may look different every day, even every hour, depending upon who is using it and for what purpose. Project processes need room, so that learners may spread out materials they use to produce authentic products. Other breakout rooms are also needed. Having a room where science experiments may be set up is necessary. Having space for an art area, a "shop" area, and a media resource center would be wonderful.

A fourth element necessary for a project-based school is to have within the infrastructure the use of modern technologies; i.e., computers, printers, scanners, video and digital cameras, media software, etc. An infrastructure ought to be established within the walls that will support learners individually creating a variety of research projects and products. The best tool to supply to the learners in these 6–12, 7–12, or 9–12 schools is to have as many computers and other support technologies as possible. Because the project-based schools do not as a matter of routine buy textbooks in subject matter for mass distribution, more money is available for computers and software that helps generate research and products. Having computers on workstations hooked up to the Internet and loaded with software that allows for research into vast varieties of information is one of the most important support tools.

Computer use in project-based schools ought to follow the ideas of Seymour Pappert (1993) and Alan November (2002): computers are tools to use, just as books and pencils were used as tools of the past. Like pencils and books, computers ought to be available to students at all times. The learner uses them as a research tool, as a word processor, and as a multimedia tool for products of their projects.

The computers, even at student workstations, ought to be Internet connected. This concept, of handing over to the learners the keys to the Internet, causes some apoplectic reactions on the part of some parents and concerned citizens. However, it ought to be recognized that in advisory groups and in open-spaced and flexible environments there is going to be adult supervision in some form. Information, as terribly wrong and antisocial as some of it is, should not be arbitrarily totally blocked from student availability. Some things, sure, but not substantial amounts.

Also, printers, cameras, scanners and the like ought to be available for learner use. If you get out of the classroom mentality and stop thinking that everything revolves around the delivery of information by the expert teacher, and that middle and high school learners are sheep to be herded, then you may be able to see the point. Alan November (2002) makes the argument that schools ought to be about *informating* rather than *automating*. The difference is great. In automating, schools use technology (computers, mostly) in the attempt to do the same routines with greater efficiency. This is only frustrating and is the reason why so many technology "plans" falter. Rather, he says, schools ought to use technology to create the means for learners to:

- "Organize poorly-structured problems while recognizing problems that no one else can see;
- Access information and people around the world;
- Understand how to be independent and interdependent, working with others (no matter where they are located) to solve problems;
- Be responsible for the quality of their work;
- Communicate their findings to audiences that will give them feedback that they can use to constantly improve their work;
- Know what they don't know and how to find resources that can inform decisions;
- Be self-organized and self-motivated so they can figure out what they need to know, and;
- Structure their own work organization and environment." (2002, Paragraph 30)

November goes on to say that "the technical skills are trivial, after all, compared to teaching people how to be free to think critically and to organize and manage the quality of their work" (2002, Paragraph 34). It is in this spirit, and around this philosophy, that the New Country School and the replica model schools integrate technology into the everyday workplace of the learner. Every school unit ought to have computers scattered around the building, at student workstations, in a resource center, in a technology center, a science project room, etc. Other technologies ought to be placed strategically so as to be used by learners and staff.

There are a variety of ways to create a project-based school out of an open space. The only thing needed is the imagination of the staff. The New Country School has the above characteristics, because it was built for those purposes. Three of the replication sites (RiverBend Academy of Mankato, Minnesota; Avalon Charter School of St. Paul, and El Colegio Charter School, Minneapolis) have leased old grocery stores or warehouse space and created what appear to be office work spaces. They also have breakout areas available for multipurpose use. River-Bend Academy, with its emphasis on the arts, has developed six arts areas out of open space, where learners can spin pottery, make jewelry, paint, weave on looms, etc.

It is neither necessary nor desirable to use old school buildings. The old characteristics stand in the way and give off the aura to learners and staff that it is school as usual. If an old school building (or new, for that matter) is to be used for a project-based school, walls of classrooms ought to be knocked out so that more open space can be utilized for advisory group workstations. More rooms should be used for specific project-producing purposes (such as an art area, science area where experiments can be carried on, a shop area) than for delivery of content to a large group.

Perhaps this all flies in the face of twentieth-century thought about schooling. As mentioned in the preface, we may have gone too far in creating cathedrals to learning, with all the costs they incur. Why can't education be carried on in open warehouses or office spaces, utilizing former business establishments? Because we have built everything around delivery of content to a quiescent, passive audience and very little around active, hands-on, adult-like behavior. And we have built up a culture of "schooling" that includes classrooms with doors (to shut out the world), gyms, corridors with lockers, etc.—places in which we can "control" the population that inhabits the building. It is time to build, or re-create, buildings for middle and high school learners that reflect the real world of adult work. For the project-based learning process, it works.

What could a school day look like in an "open school?" A suggested framework for project-based schools would be to have advisory groups meet daily as an opening session. Discussion on a variety of matters may take place, depending upon the advisor and the needs of the learners. A time to check in with young people, to find out where they are coming from, what has happened to them in the past sixteen hours since they last saw you, creates a powerful connector to the emotional aspect of a learner. To learn, they must be in a state of "relaxed alertness" (Caine & Caine, 1994). Allowing them some time to come to grips with their day-past and day-to-come will put them into such a state. An advisor could also use the time to foster ideas that may lead to projects by discussing current events, scientific discoveries, etc.

After advisory groups meet, the staff of a project-based school may decide to have a structured time for all students to do math or science projects; or, perhaps, shop and art projects. At times it is necessary to structure time around some theme, as the practitioners at New Country discovered they had to do for math. Theoretical math is one of those subjects that is difficult to build into projects; practical math can be, but what is demanded by state mandated curricula and statewide testing is a knowledge and understanding of theoretical algebra, geometry, and calculus. For these competencies to be built up, the staff decided to create a time in which all students work on their math skills, but it is done at an individual pace. They use a computer-generated program that is able to test where the learner is in their understanding of whatever subject, then generates problems for them to solve and tests on those concepts. When they demonstrate knowledge of that concept, the program generates problems in another concept. Learners are working on specific levels and areas individually, but are placed into groups to help each other. Each group also has an advisor assigned to help with basic understandings, or any problem the learner may be having with the concept.

The time may also be structured around use of a science laboratory or mechanical shop. The reason is that an adult should be in the room with the learners for safety sake. Some time is scheduled around group project time, giving groups time to meet together, or go outside of the building to pursue whatever is needed to complete a project. Many of the sites using this model have developed a silent reading time in order to get students into literature, biography, and so forth. How the time of the learner is organized is part of the "orchestrated immersion" principle (Caine & Caine, 1994). The staff, with student and parent input, may orchestrate the immersion in adult-like behaviors by creating flexible days around field trips, release time to do community service or internships, using the city library, or whatever else may be needed.

At this point the reader is probably wondering what kind of school allows students outside of the building, either singly or in small groups? The practitioners who have worked with project-based learning realize that you cannot have lack of movement in and around the community if you expect learners to have experiences with adults. We also believe in locating the building near the heart of a community, like schools used to be before they were moved beyond the hypothetical "city walls." Sometimes I wonder if adults in society really value adolescents: after all, out of sight, out of mind. It is as if adolescents are the modern day equivalent of the leper and schools the leper colonies of the past! So we place them in a building far from sight so they don't bother the "good folks" trying to carry on business. It sends a message to the youth: you are not a valued member of our society!

We believe in a school without walls, where learning takes place anywhere and at anytime. Students are encouraged to work with adults at home, in the city and in the country. What they learn from working after school hours, what they learn on family trips, or from watching TV at home, that can all be used to complete a project. The school and its personnel do not own the exclusive rights to gainful knowledge, competencies, or dispositions to dispense to learners. Rather, the advisors in project-based schools are there to help the learner make sense of, and make connections between, experiences, however and whenever possible.

In some instances learners are connected via e-mail or a website to a community expert in some area the learner wishes to know more about. In other cases, learners are involved in an internship-like experience with one of the adult members of the community. Some are carrying on community service projects in conjunction with a community social service agency. In many instances, community experts come into the building to work directly with an individual or a small group.

Part of the day may be used to allow for groups to work on group projects: to practice with a music group, to practice for a theatrical production, to plan skits, to write poetry, to paint, to work on a car, to build items of use for the school or community. When students design projects around interests and passions, anything may come up. That is the reason advisors have to have wide cognitive horizons, the ability to build the capacity for learners to control themselves, have a sense of efficacy that can be passed on, and be very flexible. Each day will not look like the day before: each day could bring a wide array of tasks for both learners and advisors.

At the end of the day it is beneficial to pull the advisory group back together again for a period of "reflection," the third and most powerful element necessary for people to learn (the others were noted before: relaxed alertness and orchestrated immersion) noted by Caine & Caine (1994). Learners can be asked to keep a journal, or fill out time-usage logs, or to reflect on the checklist of their latest project. The advisor can ask learners to reflect orally about their day. Whatever is done, reflection on what was done and how it was done is an important part of the day.

There is a way to have students participate in adult-like behaviors in conjunction with a well-designed project. The key lies primarily in the development of the learner as an intrinsically motivated person. The family-like atmosphere created by advisory groups, the personal workstations, the idea of allowing learners to construct projects around their passions and interests connected to state standards, are designed into the system to create an intrinsically motivated learner who will operate in an accountable mode. Not because they are told to, but because they see the need for acting adult-like. And they have been allowed to be in a more natural learning environment, one similar to the real, authentic world of work. Connect this with the right to design their own projects around their interests and perceived needs, and you have allowed for the development of the passionate learner, one who is learning to create their own path to adulthood.

CHAPTER 6

How Does the Project Process Work?

Creativity represents a miraculous coming together of the child with the apparent opposite and enemy, the sense of order imposed on the disciplined adult intelligence.

—Norman Podhoretz

Robert Fried in his article *Passionate Learners and the Challenge of Schooling* (2001) used a wonderful analogy to explain the paradigm shift that must occur for project-based learning to work. The shift in thinking is comparable to the shift that occurred when the world began to realize that the Ptolemaic view of the universe was no longer true, and that the Copernican view was, indeed, the real way the universe worked. The traditional system is caught in a paradigm of teacher-centeredness, where the learner must revolve around the teacher and the teacher curriculum. The project-based system, as well as brain research and constructivist theory, prefers the learner-centered universe, where the teacher revolves around the needs, interests, and goals of the learner. He uses the term *learner centered cosmology* (p. 135) to explain the concept.

The teacher-centered universe breeds the idea that the teacher is the authority figure, the dispenser of knowledge and dispensations, the person now held accountable for everything that happens in the educational enterprise. This attitude leads to the "kids versus grown-ups" effect, where the classroom becomes an atmosphere of antagonist against antagonist. Consequently, all sorts of techniques are devised to motivate and control, leading to a large industry of books on "classroom management" techniques. A learner-centered universe, however, places the onus back upon the learner to become the creator of their own path, to be the one accountable for themselves and where they are going. The professional pedagogue, or advisor, does not dictate the curriculum, but facilitates by advising the learner about the needs of society and the knowledge and wisdom of the professional educators who say that some things ought to be learned by everyone.

This learner-centered universe is the central key to the intrinsic motivation necessary to rekindle, keep alive, or create a passion for learning. By the time most children have reached middle school age, they are no longer interested in what the grown-ups have been telling them they need to learn, and have had their interests disregarded. It is necessary to begin the process of rebuilding their enthusiasm, their awe and wonderment about their world, if they are to have a meaningful journey toward a fulfilling, productive adulthood.

In order to begin a journey, a direction is needed, a goal decided upon. In a project-based system it is imperative the learner create a personalized learning plan (PLP) in order to guide them to the goal. As mentioned previously, that goal ought to be decided upon by a combination of four factors: the individual wants and needs of the learner, the goals of the parents, the goals of the professional pedagogues, and the goals of society at large. The three-way conference between parents or guardians, the learner, and the advisor determine the strengths, weaknesses, interests, and goals of the learner. A psychological assessment of learner interests, goals, learning styles, aptitudes, and weaknesses ought to be undertaken before the PLP is finalized. As mentioned earlier, the MAPP is a good tool to use for this purpose.

The project-based process is inherently a personalized process, yet one with a structure that allows for advisor and learner to interact meaningfully. Personalization of learning has been highly touted by many educators, but rarely established in the comprehensive high school setting. Personalization is based upon two things: seeing learning as paramount to teaching, and having relationships be at the center of the enterprise. The project-based system created by the practitioners at the New Country School, and practiced by replication sites, does both.

At the center of the process is the interest of the learner. The learner must begin by wanting to investigate some thing, concept, event, or knowledge base. The typical schooling process, and one that turns most high school students off, is to have a teacher-centered curriculum based on coverage and time segments. This is not the case in a purely project-based model. To begin the process, a learner must have the idea of what to study.

After discussion with an advisor, a learner may wish to investigate a topic. The advisor then sits with the learner, using a Project Proposal Form and a copy of the Profiles of Learning Curriculum Guidebook, which every learner is given when they enter the school(s). The Project Proposal Form first asks the learner to identify the topic. Then they write out at least three major questions that they hope to have answered by the project.

The learner is also asked to explain how the project will apply to life outside of school. The focus is not only on learning facts or knowledge about a curricular area, or even a thematic area, but to learn what is authentic, real, and important. Some advisors ask the learners what good the project may do them five years from now. This question also causes the learner to think about why they would want to study a certain topic, and what good it may do them in the long term. Again, authentic, real learning is the key; and the need for the learner to want to learn about the topic at the time that they perceive the need to learn it is what provides the *passion* for doing it.

The next step in the proposal process is for the learner to brainstorm a web or outline of possible topics. These could, and perhaps should, follow the Curriculum Guide's set of standards. The advisor should help the learner understand the wholeness or expansiveness of the topic, so that the learner meets as many standards in as many curricular areas as possible. Doing a web and outline allows the learner to see how topics are integrated in real life, and how arbitrary disciplines can be understood in thematic ways, not only in a linear fashion.

The learner then completes a task analysis, being asked to list the steps that are needed to complete the project and a set of timelines for each of the tasks. This forces the learner to look at the end result and how to get there. Also, the learner, with the advisors help interpreting the PLP, needs to consider their learning styles, aptitudes, weaknesses, and goals in making these determinations. The end product may be a demonstration, a display, a presentation, a reading, a slide show, or a skit. These are determined by the aptitudes and learning styles of the learner, by the curricular needs and the possible need for public demonstrations (which will be explained later). In this way learning styles are addressed very directly (unlike classroom models), in *what* is studied, *how* it is studied, and in *products* of the work. I know of no other way to directly address learning styles other than through a personalized project-based process such as this.

Along with the task analysis, the learner needs to consider resources. In the project proposal, they are asked to list at least three different types of resources: hardcopy (books, journals, etc.), electronic (Internet, TV, video, etc.), and primary sources (living people, if possible). Asking young people to contact community experts in order to ask questions about their field of expertise has proven to be a powerful learning tool. It has led to many partnerships and further investigations and projects, especially of vocations and bodies of knowledge that support the vocations. Through this use of community experts, learners begin to understand that bodies of knowledge do matter, that they are connected to real life, and that expertise in various areas does pay off in the long term. Without this "outside the walls" contact, many teens never get the connection of how classroom knowledge is authentic and meaningful.

Also listed in the project proposal are the standards the learner expects to meet when the project is finished. This exercise of looking at the possible standards to meet in a variety of fields or disciplines keeps the project from becoming either too shallow or too scattered. The way that the Profiles of Learning (Minnesota's state curriculum standards) are stated allow for an inquiry process to be utilized to understand conceptual frameworks in the various disciplines. In other words, the standards are not purely content based. This allows for project-based learning to work quite well in meeting those standards. Therefore the student-centered and student-initiated projects can be guided by them, but not dictated entirely by them. Examples of how this works will be given in the next chapter.

Finally, before the major portion of the project research and study is undertaken, the learner is asked to propose how many project credits he or she thinks the project may be worth. This gives them a goal in terms of hours and days. The practitioners have devised a project-credit basis for movement from one level to another and toward graduation. The approximate number of hours it would take to achieve one project credit is approximately 100 hours of research, writing, producing, creating, demonstrating or whatever it takes to create a worthwhile project. It would take 40 project credits in the last four years (ten a year) to graduate. These hours are kept track of by the learner and advisor, with advisors checking daily in the learner's time logs or journals.

This designation of time to the work is somewhat arbitrary, but was needed in order to give learners a good sense of what a good project was, and how much it took to really meet standards. Early in the process learners attempted to do small reports, hand in some "assignment" type of work and call it a project. When they discovered what a good project was, one that required a *passion* to be engaged in order to complete, and the time it took, better projects began to come forth. For those of you who attempt to replicate the model, you need to understand that students will attempt to "do as little as possible" and try to play the games they played in the traditional system. The "dog ate my homework" type of excuses, the "I'm working on it, but it's at home" sorts of comments; and the "I think it's good enough" statements will be put to you. But when good projects do eventually come forth, because of the time put into them, others see them and naturally want to emulate them.

When the proposal is ready, it is taken to the advisor and the review team for approval. The process calls for at least two advisors and one other adult to review the proposal. That group then becomes the assessment team for the finished product as well. At the New Country School, and at some of the replication sites, two advisors agree to work together for a year as assessors of learner's projects. Other advisors may be brought in as "experts," and are used as information resources in the process (being experts in a field as well as generalists). Parents may not sit on an assessment team for their children, but may for other learners in the school. When a proposal is ready, the advisors and other adults involved in the planning team must sign off in order for the learner to go ahead. The parents/guardians must also sign the proposal form before it is legitimized.

Having parents or guardians involved in the project proposals for their children is a powerful parent-involvement piece. There have been many attempts to increase parent involvement in schools, but none go so far as to allow parents a say in what their student is doing on a daily basis. This type of parent involvement may satisfy parents on both the right and left of the political spectrum by giving them input into the type of projects in which their children absorb themselves. There is no need to protest the curriculum. The Profiles of Learning Standards are general and process-oriented, and they allow for a variety of content to meet any one standard. So, what one student does to meet them and what another student does may be different in content, but similar in process. Parents may very well sign off on these without investigating very far, but it certainly gives them an avenue to discuss with their children what it is they are doing in school and to voice opinions on how and why they are doing it. This, I believe, is the ultimate parent involvement.

The learner is given a checklist to keep track of their project progress. Most have more than one project going at a time. This is something advisors also have to monitor. It is the nature of adolescents to get a new interest on a fairly regular basis and lose interest in some things quickly. Probably a good rule of thumb is to not allow more than four projects to be happening simultaneously. The learner has to document the time put into the projects and keeps track of various phases of the project.

In phase one, the learner needs to complete all that is necessary for the proposal to be accepted and review it with the project team. In phase two, they do the research, connect with the primary source, update the outline or web, and start roughing out the draft of the end product. In phase three, the learner will review the idea with peers, the advisor, and with parents/guardians. In phase four, they complete the rough draft, product, or presentation and review it with the advisor and the team. In all phases they are asked to complete documentation of time and learning. By the last phase, they are asked to reflect on what went well, what problems were encountered, and what they learned, especially about the standards they purport to meet. This reflection is a key to a good product and to a good assessment process for the learner.

When the learner and advisor are satisfied that everything is in order, the assessment team is called together. The learner is responsible for setting this meeting time. You may see an assessment team sitting with and assessing a student project at any time during any day in the schools. The assessment team examines the time logs and product the learner has produced, or the demonstration/presentation articles (such as a PowerPoint presentation, overheads, note cards, music/poetry written, etc.). The learner is quizzed by the members of the team about what they learned, how they learned it, what resources they used, what problems they encountered, and why they did what they did. The advisor of the learner acts as an advocate for the advisee in the process, while the other advisor and other adult may "grill" the learner. This process of using the advisor as an advocate for the learner builds a stronger emotional tie between the learner and advisor, while allowing adults to act as the "experts" and "inquisitors" for the assessment. It is a little like the "good cop–bad cop" routine in determining what the learner actually learned.

After the "inquisition," the team assigns a number of project credits (could be less than one, could be more than one) to the project and determines what standards were, indeed, met by the project. The assessment team then signs off on the proposal and project form. A grade of A–C may be assigned if the learner (and parents) desire. Usually learners begin by wanting grades, but soon learn that the process of acquiring grades is not a part of the culture. They are never averaged for a grade point average. The advisor and the learner then record the credits and standards met in their records (advisors keep records of each advisee in a secure computer program, advisees in their Curriculum Guidebook). Usually advisors create a certificate that is given to the student for their portfolio of projects.

This process is very similar to a master's thesis defense and really creates an atmosphere of formality and ceremony. Learners are rewarded richly by the process. The process also has proven a boon to the advisors, as working with each other and another adult in a variety of project topics teaches them how others interpret standards. In short, it helps standardize advisor assessment across the board. Concrete examples of this process will be given in the next chapter, along with a number of exemplary and average projects created by learners in project-based schools.

The process certainly merges the creativity and spontaneity of the child with the seriousness and disciplined mind of the adult. It has advantages over the relatively arbitrary way in which students are assessed for content knowledge in classrooms, where it is difficult to know what an "A" is in one class versus another. The process of creating and assessing projects in the project-based system is well thought out, and certainly is not a "free-for-all" that some may think an open school based on student-centered learning would use.

CHAPTER 7

How Do Projects Affect the Learners?

No one can "get" an education, for of necessity education is a continuing process. If it does nothing else, it should provide students with the tools for learning, acquaint them with methods of study and research, methods of pursuing an idea. We can only hope they come upon an idea they wish to pursue.

—Louis L'Amour

In this chapter you will find case studies of learners who were students in the school year 2001–2002. They are students at the Minnesota New Country School or at replication sites. By means of interviews and discussion, the learner's lives as students in these progressive project-based schools will become apparent. Along with understanding how learners acquire skills that will lead to life-long learning, the reader will also get a picture of projects that lead to acquiring the skills, and how projects are proposed, researched, produced, and assessed. In each of the cases presented, one project will be detailed so as to give the reader a look at the process of how learners go from an interest, to assessment of project credits, standards, and life performance skills. Other projects in which the particular learner is involved are also mentioned in order to give a view of what the life of a learner is like over time.

The number of credits for projects will be mentioned, and there will be some discussion of what state standards were met. To graduate from New Country, a learner must accumulate 60 project credits over 6 years (ten per year average). They must also show they have met 24 of 30 Profiles of Learning. In the case of most projects, learners do not meet a profile in full, but meet one portion or some portions of one. Advisors (and the learners, as well) keep track via a transcript of how many credits and profiles have been met.

The learners who are exhibited here are from a variety of backgrounds and abilities. No two are alike, yet there are similarities. Often by the time a learner has matriculated in this type of school for a number of years, it is difficult to determine whether they are special education students, what age or grade level they are, and how they did in previous schooling. Let their actions and voices speak for themselves.

Barb, age 16, first year at Minnesota New Country School

One of the learners interviewed was initially introduced to you in chapter one. Barb, who if you recall, was homeschooled in elementary, spent one year at a traditional high school, and came to New Country at the beginning of the school year. At the time of the interview she had spent only seven months at the school.

The finished project she chose to show me was one on Anastasia Romanov, the daughter of Czar Nicholas II of Russia who may possibly have escaped the family massacre by the Bolsheviks during the Russian Revolution. Asked why she was interested in the topic, Barb said the project started as a means to gain validation of standards in world history by discovering the causes of the Russian Revolution. While investigating the revolution, she became very interested in the Romanov family and the mystery surrounding Anastasia. Her passion for discovery led her to investigate the mystery, and relate it to the Revolution.

After identifying a topic, learners are asked to think of questions that they would like to have answered by the investigation. Barb identified three: who was Anastasia Romanov; is she alive and if so, where; and, why is she famous? Barb was quick to point out that this project was one of her first while at the school, and that her questions were not as in depth as in later projects.

Learners are also asked to identify how learning about the topic would apply to life in general. Barb acknowledged that knowing about other cultures would be worthwhile for her understanding of her own culture. When asked what she had learned from the project about cultures, she responded by saying she had learned about a long history of oppression, how in feudal Russian society peasants were considered as nothing, and that in revolutions lives were cheap. She said that she now appreciates our democracy, that "we don't have it so bad," and that she understood after this project why it has been difficult for Russia to create a democratic state.

The project proposal process also asks learners to identify resources they could possibly use to complete the project. They are asked to use Internet sources, hardcopy books or journals, and a living person. Barb identified some of those resources up front, but said that she found more as she went into the research. Barb started by reading history texts about Russia, but found them dry and difficult to understand. She soon found herself drawn to the Romanov saga, and began reviewing Internet sites and magazine articles about the controversy surrounding the person (Anna Anderson) who many claimed was Anastasia.

Barb then did a task analysis by attempting to set a timeline for the research and the writing of a paper on the subject. She had written in the proposal that she would attempt to meet some portions of standards in world history and culture, in communications, in arts and literature, and in historical and cultural inquiry. She proposed that the project would be only a quarter credit project. After the planning, the assessment team of her advisor, another advisor, and two other adults (in this case one of the paraprofessionals and the media specialist in the school) signed off on the proposal. Barb then took the proposal form to her parents for them to sign.

Barb's advisor gave her feedback as she processed the project over a three-month period (remember that learners do many projects at the same time). When Barb had a finished product from her research, she called together the assessment team to evaluate and assess what she had done. Barb's final product included her time log (how many hours she spent on research, organizing and writing; in this case 53.5 hours), a reflection and analysis of the process and the results of her learning, and the finished paper (which was approximately 20 pages in length). When the assessment team met, they soon discovered that Barb was underestimating her number of credits, and awarded her three quarters of a credit rather than one quarter credit. The rationale was that she had done a very in-depth paper, had presented evidences for both sides of the controversy, and had presented her view based upon that evidence.

Also, her reflection on the process was thorough. The committee could tell that she had been "engrossed in learning."

Each learner is to do a self-reflection about his or her project by using the life performance rubric, and the assessment committee either agrees or disagrees on that self-reflection. From this exercise, learners gain an understanding of the skills that lead to life-long learning. At the time this project was assessed, the school personnel still had not incorporated fully assessing learners on the rubric as a portfolio process, nor using a tracking method that would keep records of movement along the rubric. It was used primarily as a reflection. The life performance skills were discussed with parents and learners at conferences as a general guide to determine growth.

Barb has undertaken a wide variety of projects over the seven months, completing some and not completing others. Her project creating the Claymation was not completed at the time of the interview because she had to put time into another project that had a deadline. She became part of the Super Mileage Car project. In this project, a group of five is creating, from scratch, a high-mileage car to place in a statewide competition. The school had entered this contest in previous years and had done quite well. This year the team started late and had to scramble to meet deadlines. Therefore Barb put more time on that project than on others. She said "it took someone to push it — it isn't the job of the advisor to push it."

The project required the group to make plans with an advisor to schedule time for use of the shop. Barb said she "thought it would be cool" to learn about physics by doing "something fun." She had to learn to weld from the very beginning, doing a lot of discovery at the same time. Meanwhile, she has had to learn things about gear ratios, steering clearances, breaking systems, safety issues, tire and engine mounting, balance, and aerodynamics. Barb learned to do drafting last year at her other high school, and made use of it in doing the design work for the team. Barb said that it "doesn't matter what the outcome will be, I like drafting plans and it may lead to a career in design." They created written plans that were sent in to the competition committee and made a wooden model.

The process of learning by doing certainly is present in the project-based system. The advisor gave them advice, but often told the team to "go figure it out for yourself" instead of showing them exactly what to do. The team was given manuals and some organization and received some help from a welder. Barb felt that learning-as-you-go certainly is a good way to remember something you learned.

Another project Barb has been involved in is the Airplane Group. This group of learners has been planning to build a small airplane. They are presently looking over plans from various aircraft designers. Barb is involved, she says, because "it just sounds like a great idea" to create an airplane from scratch. This project, she realizes, may take the rest of her career at the school before she sees a result.

One of the first projects Barb undertook was a career investigation in veterinary science. She put about 30 hours investigating the work of veterinarians and what education was required, but is unsure she will choose the profession. She did not despair of the time and effort, though, explaining that she learned to do the proposal process, how to plan, how the project-based system worked, and so on. From this she learned that the school offered her many opportunities to explore, and she has taken advantage of that.

One of the more interesting aspects of the school is that students develop an interest in something, then organize learning groups to investigate the topic. This *self-organization principle* works well at New Country and other sites, because it allows students to come to the realization that they want or need to learn something before there is an organized method of discovery. When Barb and five others wanted to learn basic biology, they asked the life science advisor to organize a series of classes for them. The learners were given some books by the advisor, from which they chose one to be their "text." They met with the advisor once a week and asked questions (using the *questioning pedagogy* mentioned in chapter two). The advisor helped them set up lab experiments, but again, the learners had to determine the input. The curriculum is not organized around what the teacher wants to teach, but what the learners want to learn. As of this writing, the group was crossbreeding fruit flies to determine some genetic traits. Barb said, "If last year I would have been told that I would be crossbreeding flies, I would have said you're nuts." She finds this very interesting even though there is uncertainty about the outcome. As Barb put it, "if you learned something about it, it is the right answer."

Barb also finished a project regarding church confirmation. Because she was to do community service for her confirmation class, she combined that with the school requirement for community service. Barb did 24 hours of service at the school helping the advisors with inventory of science and shop equipment, helped at church dinners and events, volunteered to help the elderly, and taught first graders at Bible Camp. She also wrote a paper about confirmation that was accepted as a project meeting standards in inquiry into culture. Her paper alluded to "how cultures influence religion, especially through the family," and how our society has questioned religion. Actually, Barb decided to not get confirmed with her class because she said that she "won't do something I don't understand why I'm doing it."

The project did earn her some project credit. This is an illustration of one way the school allows for students to apply learning from any avenue, and does not subscribe to the *peculiar conceit* that students have to learn what the teachers are teaching in the classrooms in order to become good citizens. It is a good illustration showing how various other activities that teens often engage in may also become projects. The Minnesota New Country School does not discriminate as to the location where learning takes place. Travel with family, 4-H, Scouts, music lessons from people in the community, a self-designed workout and health plan, all may become validated through the project process as meeting standards.

Barb also became part of another self-organized group that met weekly to debate issues important to the group. There were ten learners who wanted to participate. They met to organize their own rules. They chose the topics. A paraprofessional aide met with them to be the referee. The group devised the rules. If a person broke the rules they could be removed from the group. The topics chosen for debate included the war on terrorism, creation versus evolution, cloning humans, drug and alcohol legalization, and the behavior of Bill Clinton. After five debates, Barb documented her research, her opinions, reflections on the process, and handed in a booklet that earned her .5 project credits. She also validated standards in inquiry into current U.S. affairs and communications.

Barb also joined the speech team at the traditional high school in the community through a pairing agreement between New Country and the local district. She did original oratory on the topic "The Negative Effects of Vaccinations in Children." To do the job, she had to research public health statistics and health science resources. She had to write the speech, then memorize it. She used Internet resources, books, journals, and the local high school coach as her resources. Barb was awarded fourth place at the sectionals, qualifying her to be an alternate to the state speech competition. She felt that New Country allowing her to use her time as her own and doing public presentations helped her improve immensely. Other than getting project credits for the contests, her speech competitions also were counted toward the state standard in speech and the number of public presentations needed for graduation.

Barb has become engrossed in a compelling number of interesting projects. But the most compelling and interesting thing about the process is the encouragement of pursuing a passion, and the encouragement of reflection. Barb certainly exuded the aura of a passionate learner in her interview. She was almost giddy with enthusiasm about her projects and about the freedom to pursue what she felt interested in at the time. Her reflections showed maturity beyond her years. In her reflections on the debates with schoolmates she mentions the necessity of sharing each other's views, "even if you don't agree." She noticed the difficulty that exists when trying to change another's point of view, especially when religion is involved. Yet she said that she appreciated the opportunity to listen to other's opinions, and felt that the group got over the attitude of disliking someone because they held a different view or belief.

In her confirmation paper, she had many a wise question, perhaps too many questions for many parents. "I need to choose, I need to decide on my own what I feel is true and right. It isn't in my nature to accept things without question," said Barb. She may very well be voicing the inner urge of every teenager in America. Giving voice to young learners, allowing them to be the questioners, allowing them to find answers meaningful to them, is the purpose of a student-centered curriculum and methodology.

Paul, age 14, second year at Minnesota New Country School

Paul is a local boy who was also homeschooled for his elementary years, and is in his second year (traditional eighth grade) at New Country.

Because of his homeschooled background, Paul and his family thought that the project-based system would be a better fit for his middle and high school experience.

Paul said that in his first year he did not understand the expectations well, even though the school puts first-year students through a "boot camp," or orientation, of one week, where they experience a teacher-led project and a pseudo project in order to learn the process. Paul said that he had difficulty understanding the depth of work and understanding needed to meet a standard. According to Paul, his first projects were "simple and not well done." The same was said for his first public presentations. In the second year, he was able to complete some unfinished projects from the first year, and he felt he understood better how to meet standards. He said that he is better at "learning what I want to do and what needs to be done to get credits and standards." He also related he was better at examining resources and knowing what he needs to get a project completed. The process, said Paul, "takes time to learn and maybe there needs to be more teacher-directed projects first."

Paul feels he made improvements in meeting standards in projects undertaken in his second year. Even though he chooses what he is interested in now, he knows that he will have to cover other topics later in order to graduate. Most projects done by Paul in his first year were not integrated, but were topical within a standard. Last year, the seventh grade year, he did more "unit classes" designed by advisors and student teachers (student teachers had to design some units in order to get credit for student teaching, as many would be going into traditional schools after their experience at New Country). These units were created to give learners opportunities to meet standards where they were needed or wanted. Again, it must be mentioned that the school designs these around student needs and desires and not teacher needs and desires. The "classes" are really more for information about possible topics, questioning, and discussion. As a result of those experiences, Paul did a dissection project. The "lab" led him and others through dissections of frogs, starfish, and pigs. Then each student did a report on some aspects of interest. Paul did a PowerPoint presentation on his dissection project, and presented it at a presentation night.

Another project done in this manner was a unit about myths. From reading about myths of the Greeks, Norse sagas, and Asian cultures,

Paul chose as a project "Dragons in Myths around the World." From these mini-course events, Paul learned how to research, glean knowledge from resources, and structure his products to the standards in the Profiles of Learning. Learners need some directional projects to get the process started, especially middle school level learners, who may not have done much in-depth research and writing before. As long as the projects offer choice to pursue some interest of the learner, they will lead the learner onto the correct path. If teachers design all early projects with little learner choice, there may be motivation problems.

The project Paul did in which he shared the whole process was called "World War II in Film." Following the project proposal process, Paul stated his interest was in the reality of events as they are portrayed in film. He also wanted to know how World War II began and ended, and why the Pearl Harbor attack drew the U.S. into the conflict. Paul believed that by doing a history project he would have more knowledge of his past through history. The resources Paul considered were recent movies about World War II, Internet resources, and people (the course advisor and group discussion, primarily). The curriculum areas that this project would partially meet were communications, interpretation of the arts, recorders of history, themes of U.S. History, literature and arts analysis and interpretation, World History and Cultures, and Human Geography. He felt that the project would be worth .5 credits.

Paul prepared a paper on what he learned. After viewing a number of recent movies about World War II, researching the Internet for reviews and documents about the events covered in the movies, Paul reached some conclusions about how Hollywood portrayed World War II in the movies. He also used the library to read about some of the events when he could not find Internet sources.

What did Paul learn, other than some facts about World War II? Two comments in his reflections on the movies: "A moment in history is impossible to re-enact no matter how many written accounts have been made. No matter how big a budget you have, it is impossible." And, "History many of the times has contradictions in the first place." It appears as if Paul has been able to learn that analyzing history is no simple thing. Quite an accomplishment for an eighth grader.

The assessment team of two advisors and another adult determined that Paul's history in film project was worth .5 credits, and he was given an "A." When asked about the grade, Paul said that he knows it doesn't mean much in the long run, but he was happy to know that the committee thought that he did a good job.

During the summer months, the advisors at New Country offer learners opportunities to participate in the advisors' "passions." Each advisor and some paraprofessionals design an activity that is fun for them and offer learners opportunities to participate in order to devise projects. For example, last summer advisors designed a bike trip, a camping event (based on the *Survivor* television show), and an archeological dig. Paul participated in the bike trip and the survivor episode. From the bike trip he was able to parlay the experience into a physical education and health project. From the survivor event, he was able to document learning in biology (they did a water sampling and ground water project during the week), and a self-designed astronomy project, which he presented.

In order to follow his interests and passions, as well as meet standards, Paul was working on the following projects:

- A community service project, where he tutored elementary students at the local elementary;
- An on-going reading project, where he expects to read 10 books by the end of the year;
- Personalized math, an on-going yearly project where he learns Algebra One via a computer program called Accelerated Math;
- A physical education–health wellness plan (he attends a local community recreation center a couple times a week, where he participates in bike riding and other sports), which he will document by the end of the year for credits and standards;
- A biography of Theodore Roosevelt (which he will present at the next presentation night);
- An economics/stock market challenge simulation, which is a group competition designed to learn the workings of the American economy and the stock market;
- A book writing project, where Paul will study famous authors in attempt to determine what makes a good short story, then he will write some of his own (this is part of his book reading project, as well);

- The orchard group, which planted hundreds of apple trees and will eventually create a student-run business; and
- Being in the school play, which he hopes to document towards partial credit for a Theater Arts validation.

Paul said that the project-based system gave him even more freedom than when he was homeschooled. He likes the fact that the advisors don't always tell him what he has to do and that he can go any route he wants to accommodate the curriculum. His parents seem to be happy with him having more freedom, yet having some input into what he is doing. Paul certainly has developed a great deal of interests and self-motivation through investigating his passions rather than learning through a teacher-ordered curriculum.

Chelsey, age 16, fourth year at Minnesota New Country School

Chelsey started at New Country when she was in seventh grade. Chelsey thought that the New Country School would offer her more opportunities to learn via a hands-on method, so she and her parents opted for the project-based school rather than the traditional school.

Chelsey said that it "took a year to figure things out," but now finds the new way of learning interesting and fun. The project she shared was one she devised to accommodate a standard she knew she needed to do, but knew she couldn't learn "from books." She is a visual and tactile learner, so needed to find ways to learn about human biology and the cardiovascular system differently. She found a resource that allowed her to learn human physiology from a homeschool resource called "The Physiology Coloring Book." Although this may seem childish from the name, the work expected of the learner is sophisticated and complex, suitable for high school age students.

When Chelsey started the project, she wanted to know about the heart and why people have heart attacks. Therefore, most of her proposal questions centered on those themes. Chelsey thought that knowing about the cardiovascular system would benefit her in her own life, but that the information could also benefit other persons by educating them about the heart. She cited the Physiology Coloring Book as a source, but also listed her family doctor and medical books as possible sources. She felt that she could meet partial standards in biology and in community health, and obtain one project credit.

The project entailed Chelsey working her way through the resource, discussing what she did not understand with the life-science advisor, and reflecting upon what she learned and how she learned it. In the process, Chelsey found she became interested in more than the heart and lungs, and she did more than she had anticipated. Consequently, when her project was assessed, she was awarded 1.25 project credits.

Chelsey reflected upon the independent learner and life performance rubrics in relation to this project, thereby using metacognitive techniques. For example, Chelsey said, "my documentation for this project was much better than it usually is for other projects." She also stated, "I was very proud of myself for coming up with a way to prove that I learned something. . . . I feel this isn't quite post high school work, but it is something that many people in high school learn about, and it has helped me understand different things about myself. For the tasks I did set for this project, I completed them when I had the deadline set, but I should, and could, have set more tasks for this project and it would have helped me get it completed sooner."

Chelsey also wrote a two-page reflection on what she had learned about the content. She commented, " Learning about science or science-related areas has never been something I've really enjoyed doing because it was always hard for me to learn it, and when I first started this project I thought that it would be the same way. It would go in one ear and straight out the other. But I was proven wrong."

Chelsey wrote commentaries on each of these chapters: respiration, kidney function, digestion, the nervous system, the endocrine system, metabolic physiology, blood and the defense system, and reproduction. The project represented learning about most of the human systems. She synthesized the information and wrote in her own words what she learned from each of the chapters. The summaries are well written and quite complete. The project certainly seemed worthy of the 1.25 credits and awarding of validations for her biology standards.

Other projects that have engaged Chelsey over the year have been: the Super Mileage Car competition, a family bike trip through state parks, serving on the Student Senate, a project on car maintenance, research into Bev Doolittle art works, the dissection project (which led her to the physiology project), and singing in a choir group. From all of these she has received or expects to receive project credits and expects to meet standards not as of yet met. Having a passion for learning has led Chelsey to learn state standards in ways that met her learning style and were very meaningful to her.

Ida, age 18, fourth year at Minnesota New Country School

Ida came to New Country as a ninth grader with a second grade reading level. Her first comment, even before I could ask any further questions, was "If I wouldn't have had this school, I would have quit." She had been in Special Education since the elementary grades, and remarked that her middle school years were very difficult for her. Being a special education student in a middle or high school is demeaning and hurtful, she said. Although special education teachers mean well, they do not have time to spend with students. Having to go to class with others, when she had difficulty reading, meant falling further and further behind and feeling more and more inadequate.

When she came to New Country, Ida was able to spend much more time with the special education teacher, who quickly realized that Ida first needed to learn to read before anything else would be accomplished. Ida was given various levels of reading as she progressed, and because the project-based system does not require classes to be attended, Ida could spend as much time as she determined necessary on her reading plan. Some days, she said, she would spend the whole day reading and working on her spelling. On other days she would spend an hour or two.

Having been given the special time and a special program to follow, Ida soon increased her reading level. In Minnesota, all students have to pass tenth grade level reading, writing, and math tests in order to graduate. Ida passed the reading test, on her sixth try, in this, her last year. Her reading level is now evaluated at the ninth grade level.

Ida stated very emphatically, "kids like me need more schools like this." The personal attention and the ability to devote time to what is really necessary are the two attributes of this model that paid dividends for Ida. In the project-based model, reading and passing the basic skills test becomes a project—an ongoing project from year-to-year—until mastery is attained.

The project Ida shared was her senior project. All New Country learners, in order to graduate, must exhibit what they have learned in a major project presented to the public. The senior project must be a 300–400 hour project, and must show that the learner has acquired the necessary research, synthesis, organizational, and presentation skills to be considered skilled enough to be a purposeful adult. Ida's senior project grew out of a mission trip she took to Mexico with a church group. While in Mexico, Ida witnessed the extreme poverty by working in soup kitchens and living with a Mexican family. Impressed with the needs of the poorer Mexican people, Ida dreamed of doing something to help.

When she returned home, Ida realized that the lives of most Americans are very selfish, and she realized how good life was to her. Although Ida comes from a lower socioeconomic background, and by and large would be considered close to the poverty level in the United States, she felt herself privileged in comparison. She had always been taught to respect what she had, and she realized she had the necessary resources to give, which primarily consisted of a big heart, willingness, and time. The time was there because she went to a school that valued doing community service and offered the time necessary to put into a major project.

As a senior project Ida chose a series of charitable activities. She asked herself three questions: how can I help save the world from poverty; how can I help to improve the world; and, how can I help make sure everyone gets something for the holidays? Ida proposed that this project would help her learn how people benefit from charities. She knew that the primary resources would be other people and their willingness to give and help. She did find, however, that it is "hard to get other people involved."

Ida came up with six various plans to help people. For the first one, because it was near the Christmas holiday and she knew people who had very little, she created the "angel tree" at the school. The angel tree is like the sharing trees that can be seen in most communities, but Ida designed the angels, each with the name of an item for a specific type of person, and hung them on the tree. She asked, through the Student Senate and announcements to the whole student body, that learners take the opportunity to help the needy. They did so by taking an angel, buying the item written on the angel, wrapping it as a present, and bringing it back to school for her to give to a needy family. All the angels were taken, and all the items were dispersed to people she knew needed them. When asked how she knew who needed the various items, she said, "I just knew." In other words, they were neighbors and acquaintances. In reflection, Ida said, "I never knew everyone in the school had such big hearts."

For her other projects Ida used as a resource a pamphlet, a guide to charitable giving, given to her by her advisor. She knew what she wanted but needed contacts and ideas to complete the project. In her task analysis she was able to select what she could accomplish in the allowed time frame in order to present her senior project in April. She also used Internet resources, where she found charitable organization contacts, and used other students, who gave her some ideas on how to complete the project. She considered meeting such standards as community service, history through cultures, world history and culture, social sciences processes, institutions and traditions in society, community interactions, and diverse perspectives.

Ida documented 300 hours of service through the six projects. The advisors and assessment committee said she had "very good information" and that she did "good work." Advisors gave her suggestions as she went throughout the process of documenting and reflecting upon what she did.

Other than the "angel tree," the other projects undertaken by Ida were:

- Sponsor a Child, where for $26 a month she is a sponsor for a poor child in Mexico. The money goes for school supplies, clothes, food, and medications. Ida finances this herself. (Ida works two jobs in nursing homes to earn money—she works all shifts, including during school hours on occasion.)
- The Church trip to Mexico and her work with the poor for a two-week experience was documented.
- Russian Care Packages, where school supplies are packed in boxes and delivered to Russian children. Other students in the school donated the boxes.
- Operation Christmas Child, where shoeboxes filled with toys, school supplies, hygiene items, jewelry and so forth, are packed for

various destinations around the world to needy families. Ida collected more than a dozen boxes from the school and community.
* Food drives, where Ida collected for various food pantries around the small towns in the area. She placed large boxes in various community businesses and the school, collected the nonperishable items, and delivered them herself to the food pantries in the communities.

When asked when she completed the charity projects, she said, "I'm still doing them, and will keep doing them." Ida did not see this passion of hers as just a means to complete credits for school. Rather, she actually lives the life of a charitable person, showing an adult-like purposefulness. Through these projects, not only did Ida complete education standards, but also showed herself to be a leader and organizer, a mediator and negotiator, a coach and facilitator, an advocate and supporter, an implementer and performer, an innovator and designer, a problem framer and solver, a producer and contributor. All of these life performance skills were shown in a high degree through these projects. In assessing learner outcomes, these skills show more value than mere standardized test scores.

Ida's other projects in her last year include:

* An on-going reading project;
* Working as a legislative page in the state legislature (where, she says, she felt out of place with the other "preppie" pages, but felt she was valued by her legislator);
* Doing Accelerated Math in order to complete basic math skills;
* An Economics project that is teaching her basic life skills, such as managing a checkbook, home budgeting, etc.

Ida has aspirations of becoming an Emergency Medical Technician, and is looking into attending a technical training institution next fall.

Ida is an example of a learner who struggled in the traditional system, but who blossomed in the personalized approach. She is the type of person who has a big heart, is energetic and friendly. It is unimaginable to think of what would have become of her if she had dropped out of the school system. There are others like Ida who come to the New Country School. There are many others in the replication sites, as well.

A well-documented case is the case of Josh, who came to New Country in his last year knowing he could not pass the state reading test. The school had the reading problem diagnosed, he and his advisor developed a prescription to follow, and he raised his level from a fourth grade to tenth grade level in less than seven months. He graduated from high school, and is now in college.

These are the types of things that are possible when a school can really personalize. That kind of personalization is not possible if the old Carnegie units, discipline-oriented classes and delivery method is held on to. The change to a project-based system can help save the lives of many young people.

Jesse, age 14, first year at Avalon Charter School

Jesse is an example of a learner from a large urban area that struggled with the large inner-city junior high schools. Jesse is also a representative of a minority group, and is included in order to show that the project-based model works with all sorts of potential learners. Jesse is in his first year (indeed, all Avalon learners are in their first year, as the school began in September of 2001) and would be the equivalent of a ninth grader. Jesse was, he says, a good student in elementary, but began to have problems when he went to a large, urban middle school. He found it hard to "fit in" when he went to the middle school, which he found very cliquish. Consequently he began to let his grades slip. He said that he could see no point to school and that they asked him to do things he "was not passionate about" (his words, without knowing the title of this book). He stopped caring, was often truant, and in trouble with his teachers. He had a number of problems with his parents, often running away from home.

When he started at Avalon, he immediately felt he was accepted. He said the school was made up of a lot of "kids like me." The school was much smaller (just over 100 students) and he found friends. As a first year learner he enjoyed exploring, but did not understand how to apply daily activities to standards. He did not document time on his explorations and was often somewhat of a handful for the advisors to keep on task.

After some time at the school Jesse learned to apply interests to projects that appealed to him. Now he finds projects he is interested in, looks at the standards, and tries to expand the project to fit the standards necessary. He mentioned that he gets so interested in projects that he spent nine hours one weekend finishing one.

Jesse shared an art project he was truly passionate about. He said he likes art and that he is a creative and artistic person. He wanted to create a sculpture after an exploration with an artist who came to the school to work with learners doing body casting. He proposed doing a papier-mâché "sculpture" of a human form. The questions he wanted answered were: how hard is it to mimic the human form; what would be the response to his sculpture; and, how long would it take? He thought that it was worth doing so that people would think about what art is. He said, "there is a lot of junk out there people claim is art. What is good art?" He hoped there would be some people who would accept his sculpture as art. In his reflection, he thought that it would not only be therapy, but also satisfy a need for recognition.

In his task analysis Jesse had to think about the resources he would use, how to make a human form, how to balance the sculpture so that it would stay upright, and what he could do with his time. He planned the sculpture with sketches. Jesse then gathered materials, created a base and found other materials he needed by "scrounging" around school. He spent 90 hours over 4–5 months to finish his artwork. He got validated standards in visual art creation and, because he did a public presentation on the work, he met a standard in public speaking. In his presentation, Jesse reflected that he had never done anything that big before, and he had trouble keeping the perspective. He was surprised that his presentation was well received—he received the highest marks across the board. He showed the advisors and the other learners that he had good presentation skills, that he could apply knowledge, was organized, and could solve problems. The art project gave Jesse a boost in morale that has led him to become self-efficacious and have a higher self-esteem than when he started at the school.

Jesse's other projects include:

- Working toward getting the city to put up a red light at the intersection where many students cross. He has written letters, visited with city aldermen and police, the state transportation department and has written letters to the editors of the major newspaper in St.

Paul. He said he is "getting the run-around," but won't stop until at least a yellow caution or crosswalk is created at the intersection.

- A Physical Education project, where he goes to a nearby YMCA to work on a personal health and wellness plan. He runs, swims, plays handball, lifts and does calisthenics on his own. He is also reading about eating healthier and what it takes to stay healthy.
- An Improv project with other learners called Comedy Sports. It is similar to the television show *Whose Line Is It Anyway?* He is writing a script for a short play or skit. He is learning staging skills and writing skills.
- Another writing project involving screenplays and scripts for possible shows, such as television or movies. He said he has 5–6 going, and he writes on 2–3 topics a day.
- A choir project with other learners. He is learning songs to sing for a presentation and music credit.
- A clothing decoration project, which satisfies his creativity and sense of fashion.
- A personalized math project in basic math, which he did not pass in middle school. He uses the computerized Accelerated Math program and is tutored by another student.

Jesse is a very articulate young man, one with a sense of who he is and what he wants. He could very well be an unhappy ninth grader stuck in a large urban high school, hating everything about what was happening to him. He gives the impression that going to a small school with other "kids like" him and having an opportunity to pursue his interests has allowed him to become an interested, passionate learner.

Kara, age 15, first year at Avalon Charter School

Kara is not a typical urban student. She may be more typified as suburban as her family lives 20 miles from the school in a northern suburb of St. Paul. Why did she come to Avalon? Kara said her middle school was too large and overcrowded. She said she did not learn anything useful. It was "all fill in the blanks and memorize stuff," she said. There were some fun classes where they "let you do stuff," but they were too few and far between. Kara also thought that the rules were too strict and the school staff "treated everyone like they were just a number." Although always a good student, Kara felt the need to look for a different sort of educational setting in order to enjoy her career as a student. She said her parents just wanted to see her happy, and knew that she wasn't happy going to the large school.

At Avalon, Kara finds more openness, more choice within the rules, and more opportunities to accomplish activities that hold her interest. For an example, she said she is going over to Hamline University (a local university that also happens to be the sponsor for the Avalon Charter School) to work with college level Biology students. She said she likes the idea that she can work with college age people and that the University of Minnesota, Hamline, and Macalaster College are all nearby. She expects to take a number of post-secondary classes while still in high school.

At Avalon, Kara said she sees her friends more often, and that teachers are like "real people you can get to know, more like friends." It appeared to Kara that the learners want to help each other more than she witnessed in other schools. This may be because of another basic principle that is inherent in personalized, project-based schools: *there is no competition for grades*, thereby no tracks or classes of people. Consequently, there are fewer cliques based upon "achievement." Why would learners not help each other? There is nothing lost in being a helper. This phenomenon of learners being helpful to other learners is apparent in all the project-based schools in the replication sites.

Kara's very first project was a career exploration project. Her choice was to satisfy the standard, but she also had a great interest in becoming a veterinarian. She had a part-time job with an animal clinic, where she cleaned cages, fed animals, comforted animals during shots, and did some computer check-out for customers. Kara wanted to know what skills were needed to become a vet, what kind of education and experience was needed, and what are the expected tasks. She saw this as having a direct application to her possible life's work, and she wanted to know how she could benefit society. Kara did a web, linking all the roles and possible areas to investigate. She listed the steps necessary to research, interview, work at the clinic, look at her personal skills and interests, develop goals for herself, and do the bibliography. Her potential resources, and ones she did use, were the Internet, books, and interviews with veterinarians. The standards she would meet would be in career investigation. She did not try to fit in other standards. She decided to write a paper, probably out of school habit, she recognized.

In her reflections, she noted she had increased her research skills, her communication skills, that the project went smoothly, and that she was satisfied with what she had done. She was awarded .5 project credits and received an "A." Kara does not ask for grades on all her projects, but did so on this one.

On the life performance and independent learner rubrics, Kara reflected about her project, and gave herself high marks on almost all categories. Her advisors agreed. It was obvious that Kara is capable of being an independent learner and needs little goading or guidance.

Other projects Kara became involved in include:

- Accelerated Math, where she finished Algebra I in four months, and is now approximately half finished with Geometry, possibly finishing this year. She is happy with the program and the personalized means of learning math. This shows what a good learner can accomplish when a school curriculum is not a hinderance.
- A reading project where she is part of a Book Club, a self-organized group of learners who read, meet, discuss various literary works. She has read between 10 and 15 books, and is reading things she "never thought" she would read. The learners submit reflections to advisors for assessment of the literary analysis standard.
- A community service project that includes school clean up and serving on the All School Congress. She serves on committees having to do with field trips, school improvement, and student-advisor relations.
- Taking a German seminar with a visiting scholar. They meet three times a week, use a workbook, are tested on vocabulary and concepts, and then progress to other parts of the workbook. Kara will also attend a German festival at a local college. She is presently creating a poster that will describe the geography and natural habitats of Germany that she will present at a presentation night.
- A garden project, restoring her back yard to a native habitat. Kara has been researching prairie habitats and expects to plant native plants and flowers in the spring when the weather permits. She

expects to have learned about biology and environmental preservation.

- A world literature project, where Kara practices analyzing various short stories, poetry, and fiction. She is accomplishing this with a friend, and will work with an advisor who has the background in literature. This may be an on-going project.
- A physical education and health project. Kara designed her own plan for fitness, using the nearby YMCA for workouts. She is also researching exercise and cardiovascular and muscular systems to learn human biology.
- A Latin project, which is similar to the German project, but does not have the visiting scholar on a regular basis. Kara says she is just beginning to learn the basic vocabulary, but already sees how knowing Latin could benefit her knowledge of English.

Kara has not done much with computer technology as of yet. She knows how to use the Internet for basic searches, and knows how to use the word processing applications. She expects to learn other applications in the next three years.

Kara is "really happy" with the school and thinks it "is the best thing that happened" to her. She expects to go abroad either her junior or senior year to study, but to come back to graduate from Avalon.

Mark, age 17, second year at RiverBend Academy

Mark is another learner who was on a course to failure in the traditional system. He also was struggling in his first months at RiverBend Academy, a project-based school of 150 students in Mankato, Minnesota. But since the first half of last year until near the end of his junior year, Mark has been a "star" learner at RiverBend.

Mark is a product of a mixed ethnic background, therefore considered a minority in Mankato. After not performing in the two junior and high schools he previously attended, Mark admits he came to River-Bend looking for an "easy way." He did not perform in the classroom settings, with time restraints and teacher-led curriculum.

He thought that maybe he could "get away with not working" at another school. After about three months, following a heart-to-heart talk with his advisor, Mark began to realize that if he wanted to be something, he was the one responsible for making it happen. He had to learn to set goals and work with others in an open setting. This took awhile, as most of his previous experience was as a passive learner. At River-Bend, he discovered he had to work to get credit, and the change did not come easily.

After he took charge of his learning and his life, Mark began to look into colleges, scholarships, and financial aid. He has set ambitious goals for himself. Mark has been a self-proclaimed video game junkie for quite some time. He learned through the project-based methods used at River-Bend that he could pursue this passion as a learner and for a possible career. His major project to this time, the one Mark has the most obvious passion for, is developing a video game. In this game, Mark and his cohorts (he is doing this as a group project) developed characters, settings, and obstacles to overcome in a video game of some complexity. Mark researched websites and read books and magazines on video game creation to get ideas and the know-how to program software. The project required use of media, graphic, and modeling software. Mark and his friends learned mostly from experimenting and "just doing it."

In proposing the Video Game Design project, Mark asked the following questions: what kind of software is needed to create a digital map; what kinds of weapons can we create; what kind of story line do we need; and, what is the point of the game? The purpose in creating the game was to better understand the technology and how to use it to create games, models, movies, and animations in order to become proficient. Mark mentioned that his main goal in life is to work for Lucas Arts (headed by George Lucas, of *Star Wars* fame).

Mark created a web of what he needed to do for the project. He listed as needs the ability to understand and use Adobe PhotoShop, Movie Intro, Flash 5, 3D Max, and G Max software. His tasks included drawing maps, models, and weapons; developing characters; developing a rough sample of the game; and then complete the game for presentation. His resources listed were the Internet websites, downloadable software, editing programs, and technical books.

The standards that Mark could partially fulfill with this project included some portions of technical applications, computer applications, discrete mathematics, technical writing, and literature and the arts. The final product was a playable PC video game that could be an introduction to an animated movie. In the assessment, Mark demonstrated to the committee of advisors and adults how he made the game and how to play the game. As a result of the documented 5000 hours he put into the development of this very sophisticated game, Mark was awarded 6 credits.

This project led to Mark's awareness that he should pursue computer graphics and design for a living. He researched requirements to obtain scholarships at computer graphic art and design schools in New York City and San Francisco. He considered possible scholarship and competition possibilities. This project, obviously, was not just another project. The project became a defining moment for Mark. He is making the transition from use of amateur software to professional software. Interestingly enough, two of the friends who collaborated with Mark on the project are themselves high school students at another high school in the area. They did it for the passion, but they got zero credit for working on this because it is outside of their curriculum.

Mark's other projects include:

- A history project on Auschwitz and World War II;
- Learning *html* to create websites and to satisfy a second language requirement;
- A health-physical education fitness program;
- Continuing with Algebra II via a group/class;
- Working with a group to develop a Kiwanis Key Club at the school. Mark is creating a website for the school Key Club and the regional tri-state unit. Mark will be attending the international Kiwanis Club conference in Anaheim this summer, for which he is organizing fund raisers;
- He expects to parlay a summer camping trip to Wisconsin into a health/PE and geography project for next year.

Mark has seen many good things happen to him and others since enrolling at RiverBend Academy. He is upset about the negative connotations the school often is beset with, such as being a school "for losers." He says it is just another way to be educated which fits his, and others', learning styles.

CONCLUSION

All the learners in the schools show a passion for what they are doing. They have told us that the schools have made a difference in their lives. Are they aberrations, or are they typical? I believe you could find stories like this from any of the learners in any of the project-based schools. It certainly is possible to find such stories in any school, as long as one teacher showed an interest in any one student. But all the learners I have talked with over the years say similar things about these schools.

Although not a typical learner, Kara is an example of what can happen to free the spirit within by allowing learners to attend to their interests. Barb is another who would probably exhibit the appearance of being successful in the traditional system, but who has blossomed into a happy, gregarious, self-efficacious learner. Paul would possibly be a successful student in any venue. All three, Barb, Paul, and Kara, appear to be grasping for every kind of learning experience possible. It is apparent to any person that would talk with these young people that they are are engaged and that they love what they are doing.

Ida, Jesse, and Mark were classified as having some special needs, and all found success via the personalized approach. Jesse and Mark had needs more in the emotional area, and Ida's in the cognitive area, but all have made strides in becoming the people they were able to be. Ida exhibits the heart of a philanthropist, Jesse the soul of an artist, Mark the technical talents of a professional. All three could have been lost if they had remained in a traditional school.

Chelsey perhaps represents the middle ground. She may have remained an average student in the traditional system, but without great aspirations or great interests. It is difficult to say. It is not possible to know for sure what would have happened. All we know is what has happened, as attested to by the words and works of the people who have been through the change.

When hearing stories of the young learners who have been through some of the changes exhibited here, there is always something that comes to my mind: the medical practice credo that says, *first, do no harm*. It appears that the natural style of learning, the exploration and discovery that we all experienced when we were toddlers and preschoolers, is upset by the mass schooling methods used. As attested to by the above narratives, the factory-style, depersonalized method does do harm. It limits the spirit of inquiry and the passion for learning.

For all of the learners mentioned, it was necessary to change how education was done for them to feel successful, challenged, and fulfilled. Is the project-based method the only way to do that? Possibly not. But it allows for personalization, personal space, choice, greater relationships with teacher/advisors and other adults, greater opportunities to create family-like relationships with other learners, and for interests to surface. No greater role for education can be found than to allow the passion for learning to come to life.

CHAPTER 8

How Can You Overcome the Obstacles?

The kind of schools we need would help students gradually assume increased responsibility for framing their own goals and learning to achieve them. We want students eventually to become architects of their own education.

—Eliot Eisner

Having a school in the manner and format conducive to project-based learning and that creates a passion for learning, is best done by creating a new school. Reforming an already existing school is very difficult. There are major obstacles to overcome. Although some schools have converted to charter status and/or made significant changes, it is because the school had staff members that saw the need to make the changes and found converting the best way to do so. Some large high schools have, or are in the process of, creating small units out of one large unit to affect options and choices of varieties of learning formats. There are high schools across America (usually small) that have made significant changes in their programs to some forms of project-based learning, service learning, or place-based learning. Many have had similar successes as the Gates-EdVisions sites.

However, we have found that utilizing the charter laws in the states that have such laws is the best way to affect change to a radically different learning program such as pure project-based learning. Although this manner does not fully fulfill the vision noted in the preface to this book, it is the place to start. The charter laws were established in order to affect change in two ways: to provide competition so that loss of students would force traditional schools to adopt new methods; and to provide research and development sites so that innovations may be studied for their effect on student learning. Although ten years old, the charter laws and charter schools are still under fire from the established order in education, and still are beset with political and financial problems. But some research shows that many schools have met their conditions for their charter: they have proven they help many students achieve who were not achieving otherwise; and they have tremendous parental and student support. Charter schools have more autonomy, in that they have more control over "purchasing, hiring, scheduling, and curriculum" (Bulkley & Fisler, 2002, p. 5) than traditional school sites. Charter schools generally utilize more testing of students and are more directly accountable to parent and student needs than traditional schools (Ibid.). Although some charter schools are not much more innovative than other schools, chartering more easily allows for the type of innovations discussed in the previous chapters. Most of the successes may be due to the fact that most charter schools are small, rather than they use a particular learning model. However, the project-based system pioneered at the Minnesota New Country School and at replication sites has proven to be a great option for providing the learning-to-learn skills, the inquiry skills, and even the basic skills necessary for productive adulthood.

If the previous examples and theories mentioned have caught your attention, and appear to be a worthy program to adopt, then I suggest you do everything possible to affect the necessary changes to provide the program in your community. Your children will love you for it. It will not be easy. There is much to overcome. But it is a worthy effort.

There are a number of traditional assumptions about education that need to be overcome when considering such major changes in delivery and governance. The first general assumption is that all stakeholders and the general public know what learning is. This leads to the assumption that education as it has been perpetrated upon the unsuspecting public for the past 100 years is as it should be. The reason that this book begins with discussions on what learning and assessment are is because of the need to dispel that assumption. Learning is not what we had always assumed, nor is it what the traditional system continually espouses. It is more than learning the three R's, especially in the latter stages of middle and high school.

A second general assumption to overcome is that all children will learn and do learn the same discrete pieces of knowledge at the same time, in the same way and at the same rate. We know that is not true, yet it has become a cultural icon due to the factory system and management of large numbers in the same setting. It is also a product of the felt need to create discrete disciplines that need to be imparted by traditional delivery methods. Neither of these assumptions is supported by research, and they need to be pointed out as merely assumptions, not realities.

A third assumption is that if teachers teach it better, all will learn it better. For years educators have looked toward various reform methods to enhance their delivery, but have not been terribly successful because they refuse to change the basic underlying system. People need to see that it may well be the overall system that needs changing.

A fourth assumption is that the more course offerings, the more options that are offered, the better the school. What most people forget is that students can only take so many of those courses anyway, and that within the course offerings, there is rarely any choice beyond teacher-directed curriculum. The courses are all time based and coverage is often the overruling element, therefore students rarely can get into a topic in depth.

Another assumption is that large, comprehensive high schools need principals and superintendents to deal with the day-to-day management of students and personnel. Only if they are large, and only if they are organized into the factory models that now exist. What if schools were organized differently? Challenge the public assumption that large schools are needed to help young people learn the skills required to become a purposeful adult.

A corollary assumption is that to have good schools, there is a need for good teachers to become principals and superintendents who have vision and talent, and that you have to pay megabucks to get them. Again, only if you need managers in a large, factory-like schools. This also means that principles and superintendents are foremen and teachers are workers. Teachers are always relegated to a status of employee with very little say in the operation of the school. This assumption needs to be challenged because teachers need to be decision makers, as they are on the front lines with the learners every day.

And finally, the assumption is made that if principals and superintendents are good leaders, teachers will teach better, students will learn better, and scores on standardized tests will be higher. Hence the need for leadership programs, credentials, institutes, etc., that take good teachers away from the students. This also places a great deal of pressure on the leadership and causes many a principal and superintendent to leave positions due to stress.

All of the above assumptions are due to the development of *school-as-usual* as a cultural icon, one that must remain the same because, for lack of a better reason, it is the way it has always been done. Therefore, the first obstacle to overcome is a cultural view. Traditional school remains as it is because it is usual and common. Almost everyone has gone through a similar program, therefore it *is* education. Having been taught in the orientation one manner, with a teacher in charge of curriculum, directing memorization of facts, utilizing textbook worksheets, and assessing with paper-pencil tests, it is easy for most people to see it as normal. When people hear of doing school differently, with student-directed projects and teachers as generalist-advisors, it generally does not conjure up a picture of a rigorous learning experience. It sounds like too much fun, and if it is fun it can't be meaningful learning!

This is why different types of learning were referenced in chapter two. It must be understood that mere memorization of factual information is not the only type of learning. Doing and being are important, too. If learners can be given the opportunity to learn how to do research, accomplish long-term projects, and create new knowledge they have a chance of being more purposeful adults. This point must be made in order to have an opportunity to create a project-based program.

Part of that cultural tradition is young people being asked what grade they are in, and having special things organized around this idea of class. Because of the *peculiar conceit*, learning outside of school is not recognized. Lives of junior and senior high students are highly controlled. Through sports, music programs, theatre and the arts, student activities are controlled through the schools. School is a major cultural institution that arouses feelings of expectations similar to those aroused within a religious tradition. And school culture is just as difficult to change as a religious ritual.

The economics of school are also aligned on the side of typical school-as-usual. Students are expected to buy tablets and pencils and backpacks for their textbooks, to buy special clothing deals during "back to school" sales, and are expected to "go back" to school in the fall. Textbook companies make huge amounts of money in selling books organized around the disciplines and classes of students. State funding formulas support the standard delivery system. Master contracts support teachers teaching as they always have. And now testing services are making huge amounts of money with standardized testing becoming a national norm. The economic power structure is in the hands of the traditionalists.

Yet, if people were quizzed as to what were their most meaningful learning experiences, they would more than likely say they consisted of extracurricular activities, out-of-school field trips, and hands-on activities. Very few remember what they were "taught" in high school. They only remember the relationships and the fun things they did. Yet the general public cannot give up the idea that all of what they have forgotten is so very important for everyone else to experience. What do you say to this?

The best thing we have found to overcome this generalization is to visit a site that utilizes the form and function of project-based learning. After seeing how it can work, most people say they would have loved to be in that atmosphere for their learning. It is so much more a real world situation. To create a school of the nature of the Minnesota New Country School, or El Colegio, or Avalon, or RiverBend, the most powerful element is to have skeptics see how it operates. This is why the New Country School has hundreds of visitors a year.

People need to see that learners can be productive and purposeful in what may be termed an open atmosphere. The daily lives of learners are not entirely free to do as they please, although they have a great deal of latitude in designing their day-to-day operations, just as they would if they were in the workforce. This must be stressed to overcome the cultural attitude of what schooling ought to be. Show them that the atmosphere is such that learners learn what it is like to live in the real world, not in the artificial one of typical school.

One visitor, a university professor, wrote the following e-mail after her visit to the New Country School:

> The words I heard from your students made the most profound statement about the education they are experiencing. Repeatedly, I encountered students who spoke of their ability to follow their passion or were allowed the freedom to explore their ideas fully while still meeting the educational requirements of the state. One student commented that students from the school could perform at the level of any other school on a standardized test but in addition, students at the New Country School received life skills far beyond those provided in regular K–12 environments. As I spoke with students, they were very comfortable and mature as they spoke of their aspirations, skills, and interests. In fact, their ability to dialogue about their education with a complete stranger seemed foreign to me given my experience in secondary schools. The skills (e.g., project completion, self-direction, time-management, goal setting) the students were learning and developing seem to fit the "real world" in a much more profound sense than our typical assessments in the K–12 school years. Watching and listening to your students provided validation of my beliefs about education.

Testimonials such as this are quite common from visitors. The atmosphere should be seen and visitors should talk with the learners. Talking with the learners is what hooks most visitors. They can easily see the passion and protectiveness that the program builds in the students who participate.

Just as the general public accepts the culture of typical school, even more so for the people who work in the system. It is very difficult for a teacher or principal to view schooling as anything different than what they deal with on a daily basis. This has been ingrained in them from the days of their schooling, and reinforced during their teacher preparation and/or leadership training. Even though preparation programs mouth the words of constructivist philosophy, and have novice teachers read about and discuss orientation-two and orientation-three teaching, they all end up student teaching with traditional teachers who utilize mostly orientation-one methods. Naturally, they see this as the "way it is done."

Yet, educators who know that many children are not served well under the typical, traditional way of doing things created the project-based system. Many educators know that they have to really get to know their students in order to help them. Many secondary educators know that if they had time to personalize for students they could do better by them. Many know that if they could get technology in the hands of students, they would become more motivated. Most educators believe that students need to learn how to learn and that they all learn better when a passion for learning is present. Yet, they hold on to their *peculiar conceit* of expecting students to know their subject, and traditional ways of doing things, because they cannot conceive of ways to integrate disciplines and personalize within the system. They have to learn that there is a way to get around the system, that systemic change is possible in order to do good things for young people. Change is difficult for everyone, but more so when the general culture of a system or the public at large does not see the possibilities. We must make the possibilities seem real.

Changes made in the system too often are merely tinkering around the edges. One metaphor that seems to fit is "reconfiguring the airplane while it is still in flight." You can change pilots, you can change the number of seats, change who serves the clients, even offer a variety of drinks and snacks. But in the end it is the same airplane. Only when you get grounded and start over can you create a different flying machine. Tinkering with minor reforms takes too long and too many learners are being lost. It is necessary to see that the system can be changed, that small neighborhood schools, with generalist advisors and with real world student work, is possible. Then you must convince the parents and educators in your community.

A major mind-set to overcome is that charter schools are hurting other public schools, that they are run by unstable people with fly-by-night ideas, or even that they are private schools. Or, as was mentioned early on in the movement, that they will take all the best students and educators (which would seem to indicate that they are worthy schools)! School board associations, teacher's unions, and associations of administrators have all worked to stop or moderate the growth of charters. The reason given, primarily, is to keep the public system strong. Many educators truly believe that the traditional way is best, and I have no problem with that. But another reason may be to save their power and influence in the present system. If that is the reason, it is not good enough. Young people come first.

One thing I can say from my experience, charter school educators are some of the most caring and giving in the field. The risk of loss of security and the time and effort taken to create and run your own school are two good reasons not to do this. But the rewards are great, and heartfelt educators all across the country have taken that risk. Find educators who you know love to work with adolescents, who have done active things with students, who know that they can do better in different circumstances. Form a coalition with them and with community leaders to get the changes made.

It is not the purpose of this book to give the reader all of the statistics and rationale behind chartering. Information is available in almost every state. It is the purpose, though, to elucidate the methods needed to create a project-based system. If working through the present school board, administration, and local teacher's union can get the changes done, then go for it. If not, then make an end run around the system, if your state allows for that to happen.

To overcome the stigma attached to charters you will need a very good public information plan. Public meetings ought to be organized so that the information can be disseminated. Always take the "high road" in these meetings. Never bash the public system, as it does serve a purpose and a large number of students. You are providing a choice for educators, parents, and learners who have felt a need for a different way of learning and teaching.

The primary audience for your information sessions will be parents of children who have struggled in some aspect of school. These could be students who have been diagnosed for a special education classification and whose parents feel they are not well served. They could be students who do not feel safe in a large high school, and who want attention in a large school. They could be students who want more access to computers and technology than is typical in the system utilized in traditional schools. Or, parents of young people who know their sons and daughters learn best by hands-on activities and doing things outside the school walls. And many homeschoolers are looking for a way to have the public education system serve their needs. These are generally the clients who will listen and who will try a school that is different. Welcome them to your meetings and they will help recruit others to the movement.

Business people in the community are good allies. Generally they can see the need for a project-based system, as they understand that is how most of the world works. When they understand that young people will be partners in community development, that young people will be gaining the learning-to-learn skills necessary to be good employees and creative managers, they will come on board to help. Other professionals in the community may also see the necessity for having a project-based school that creates an atmosphere of enthusiasm. Local politicians should be cultivated, especially if they were voted for and backed a charter law in the state.

It is necessary to have a good coalition of the public in order to overcome the inertia of large bureaucratic institutions that education has fostered in the past 100 years. But it is also necessary to have educators lead the movement. Teachers who see the need to do things differently, usually those who have utilized orientation-two practices and see the need to go a step further, are the spearhead for the movement to develop a new school or change the old. Teachers, parents, and local leaders should all be involved in changing public perceptions of what a learning community can be. It has been done in a number of communities; it can be done in yours.

Teacher leadership is necessary so that new ways of learning and teaching can be explained. In most cases the new project-based schools will be led by and controlled by the teachers. If the teachers are added to the program after the initial vision and mission have been established, you run the risk of having teachers in the school who do not share in that same philosophy of education. Part of the mission and vision of project-based schools, especially charter schools, asks the teachers to organize and manage the school's day-to-day operation. The ones who had the idea to make the shift to project-based learning will be the most committed ones to the success of the school.

Teacher leadership of this notion is very unique. Yet without the teacher leadership the model does not give the learners the true modeling of real life, either. Part of the mission of the founders of the New Country school was to create a means by which teachers could also control their own destiny. Not only were the learners to have their interests and needs met but so were the teacher-advisors. Choices and control of destinies, along with accountability, are inherent in the whole system, from learners to parents to advisors. The schools being created by the Gates-EdVisions Project ask that the teacher-advisors develop individual responsibility, accountability, and ownership of the educational process. In the top-down management systems in large traditional school districts, teachers have very little control over their enterprise.

It was in this light that the founders of the Minnesota New Country School created a teacher-owned cooperative in order to form a professional practice organization to have control over personnel and curriculum. The cooperative invites teachers and support staff to become members of the organization in lieu of hiring them. The cooperative then presents a contract to a school board to provide the program and the personnel. The professional organization is responsible for seeing to it that professional development plans are carried out and that staff evaluation is done by peers, parents, and learners. In this format, administrative duties are carried out by either the advisors themselves as extra duties or the professional association hires administrators. This makes administrators subject to the teacher-advisors, rather than vice versa. This leaves the teachers in complete control of daily operations.

Parents are naturally involved in the project-based program (see chapter 6), but they can also be a part of the local professional organization, thereby having a part in personnel and curriculum management decisions. Having such an organization can provide a democratic voice in the operation of a school program.

The idea of outsourcing the personnel and curriculum may seem strange. Yet schools outsource a large number of other functions: school lunch, bussing, psychological services, etc. Why not teachers? This arrangement in public education is very new and is not legally supported in many ways. Union contracts, which keep the teachers in position of employees rather than professionals, are upheld through master agreements. The arrangement only exists in the charter sector as of this writing. However, in the future it may be possible to have regular school districts make such contracts with teachers, giving teachers true control over their professional duties.

It is not necessary to create a professional teacher's organization in order to accomplish the changes to a project-based system. It may be done through regular channels of change (i.e., local school boards, local administrators, and local union members). If a majority of teachers in a traditional system want to affect such changes, they can do so. It will, however, require a great deal of time, effort, and possibly extra funds. But the airplane is grounded every nine months for a term of two to three months. If teachers and administrators are willing, the flying machine can take on a different shape during summer months.

Small, rural high schools in danger of losing students to a large, comprehensive high school in a regional center may also need to take a good, long look at the project-based, teacher-run schools. The Minnesota New Country school, which has no administrator, seven advisors, and one special education licensed teacher, carries on a full curriculum and offers all kinds of opportunities for learners. It is even a more full curriculum if you look at the sources of projects. New Country, with an advisor as the business and finance manager, with a teacher-owned cooperative providing services, has operated in the black as well. It is possible to be small *and* efficient, if the whole of the system is considered. It is not possible to do when holding on to some of the old system.

It is necessary to see that learning is more than just acquiring factual knowledge. It also is necessary to see that you can reconfigure the places where schooling is done into small, neighborhood schools. It is necessary to see the possibility of having a successful high school without "covering" all the disciplines and reorganizing the way teachers teach. It is necessary to believe and understand that for learners to be successful in the future, they need life-long learning and technology skills. If you can buy into these things, then it possible to create a project-based school.

If you want to see results like the project-based schools are seeing in developing a passion for learning, learning-to-learn skills, and skills for a purposeful adulthood, then it is worth attempting. Education is all about the learners. Think outside the box. Do what is best to keep the passion for learning alive. It is well worth it.

2001–2002
Project Proposal Form

Name: Date:

Names of others if group project:

_____   _____   _____

Title of the project: _____

I. Identify the topic to be researched and/or investigated:

II. List at least three basic information/fact questions you would like to answer concerning your project.

    1.

    2.

    3.

    4.

III. How does your project apply to life outside of school? What makes this project important to the community/world around you? (At least two reasons)

    1.

    2.

    3.

IV. Brainstorming **(May choose between A and B or do both)**
  A. Develop a Web (Attach)
  B. Design an Outline (Attach)

V. Tasks/Activities to complete this project: Date to complete by:

_____   _____

_____   _____

_____   _____

_____   _____

_____   _____

_____   _____

VI. List a minimum of three different types of resources you will use. **At least one of these must be a primary source (living person).**

    1.

    2.

    3.

    4.

VII. List the Profiles that will be validated after project completion. **(Need to have the applicable profiles copied, highlighted and attached to the proposal form.)**

VIII. Number of Proposed Project Credits **(Must have documented hours/work to receive credit.)**_____

IX. *Initial Proposal Approval:*

Parent/Guardian: _____   Date: _____

Advisor:_____   Date: _____

Project Planning Group:

_____   Date: _____
_____   Date: _____
_____   Date: _____

X. **Checklist needed to be completed before final approval.**

a. Documentation of Project Learning   _____
b. Timelog   _____
c. Project Checklist (If needed)   _____
d. Works Cited/Bibliography(example   _____
found on page 276 of Writers Inc.)
e. Performance Rubric   _____
f. Summary/Reflection (Describe the   _____
process of completing. What went
well and what would you do differently?
How did the project affect you as a
student, citizen, and/or family member?)

XI. *Final Approval:*

I agree my child's project is ready for final approval.
Parent/Guardian: _____   Date: _____

Advisor:_____   Date: _____

Project Planning Group:

_____   Date: _____
_____   Date: _____
_____   Date: _____

 # Documented Hours: _____
Actual Project Credits: _____
Letter Grade: _____

Performance Rubric for
Minnesota New Country School

Basic Project Skills: (Evaluate with each project)

Documentation of Time and Learning	All learning efforts and time completely documented with journals, pictures or other methods including description of activities, problems and successes.	More than 1/2 of the learning efforts and time documented.	Less than 1/2 of the learning efforts and time documented.	Basically no learning efforts and/or time documented.
Tasks	The student will generate a thorough list of specific tasks for project completion.	Student generates over 1/2 of the tasks necessary for project completion.	Student generates less than 1/2 of the tasks for project completion.	Advisor generated task list for project completion.
Project Assessment	Student is able to assess his/her own work **and** generate rubrics/assessments for his/her own work.	Student is able to assess her/his own projects, but needs help creating or just doesn't create rubrics for assessing.	Student needs help in determining the quality/understanding of their own work.	Student shows little concern for work quality and is just doing the work to get it done.
Project Quality	Professional Quality-No blemishes, flaws or mistakes. Marketable.	Post HS Quality-Excellent piece but less than Pro. Limited market.	Good High School work. Acceptable work for graduation. For mom.	Numerous blemishes, flaws and mistakes. Aim higher and try again.
Resources	Use at least three different **types** of specific resources including one live (primary) expert.	Use at least two different types of resources that includes a live (primary) expert.	Use at least one resource.	No resources used.

(continued)

Ownership	Generated own idea, model, process, and product.	Adapted model to own interest and idea came from elsewhere.	Independently followed the model as given and made some personal choices. Followed model with supervision.	No personal interest reflected in project. Others gave student idea for project.
Task Completion	Time deadlines are set for all project tasks and completed within time goals (revised or original).	Deadlines are set and completed within time goals for more than 1/2 of the project tasks.	Deadlines are set and completed within time goals for less than 1/2 of the project tasks.	No deadlines are set and/or tasks completed on time.

Critical Thinking Skills: (Evaluate with each project)

Comprehension	New facts gathered when needed, gathering those facts provides leads to getting more information.	Realizes the need to gather information, but needs prompting to get more information when needed.	Gathers facts when told to.	No new information gathered to produce a quality project.
Competency	New things were created or new thoughts developed based on the new information.	The new information is applied to at least one new situation.	Much of the new information is remembered/memorized.	New information is gathered but very little or none is retained.
Context	Information/knowledge used in multiple "real" contexts.	Information/knowledge used in one "real" context.	Information/knowledge used in a contrived context/situation.	No context is applied to learning.

(continued)

Life Performance Skills: (Evaluate with each project)

Leader & Organizer	*Others Follow *Has Vision *Gets results *Others Respect *Effective use of time *Effective prioritizing *Follows through *Delegates	*Starting a following *Visions has structure *Leadership efforts with little success	*Vision starting *No followers *No real attempt at leading *Goals- no follow through	*Negative effect on others *No goals
Mediator & Negotiator	*Is sought out to help resolve a problem *Articulates the sides/issues that lead to a solution *Demonstrates respect (open-minded, active listener)	*Listens *Knowledge of subject matter *Fact-based communications *Motivated to find practical solutions	*Attempts solutions without all the facts *Has facts but unable to implement in a useful negotiation *Doesn't get involved	*Agitates the situation
Coach & Facilitator	*Assists others to meet goals *Sticks to goals *Encourages others	*Mentors by example *Willing to coach, but still developing skills to engage others	*No mentoring, coaching or facilitating happening	*Interferes with other students' learning
Advocate & Supporter	*Go to bat/ stand up for someone publicly *Handles confidential information wisely	*Other-centered *Support others individually	*Indifference *Self-centered	*Not confidential *Gossips/degrading/malicious *Not accepting of other's ideas

(continued)

Implementer & Performer	*Positive effect on audience *Demonstrates high achievement and effectiveness in presentation *Able to accept and apply constructive criticism *Creates relationship with community	*Demonstrates discipline in preparing for successful presentation *Fulfills requirements of presentation night adequately *Able to accept constructive criticism	*Can demonstrate learning *Needs more preparation or practice for public *Difficulty accepting constructive criticism	*Unwilling or unable to demonstrate learning
Problem Framer/Solver	*Demonstrates ability to solve complex (real life) problems	*Solves simple problems *Offers solutions that don't work	*Perceives a problem but there is no attempt to personally solve the problem	*Doesn't see the problem
Innovator & Designer	*Original Work *Creates/invents something new/unique *Willing to take a risk even if you fail	*Modify existing plans *Try new ideas sometimes with no final product	*Use someone else's plans/design *No inventing or designing *Assisted in someone else's innovation/design	*Plagiarizes *Stealing other's ideas *Mom or dad do it for you
Producer & Contributor	*Professional quality products *Few blemishes/nearly perfect *Consistently making positive contributions to community/school	*High school quality products *Generally provides positive contributions	*Product quality needs help but shows hope *Little or no contribution	*Student shows little concern for quality *Provides negative contributions to groups or community

(continued)

Skills not necessarily related to specific projects: (Evaluate at least twice per year)

Time Usage	Working on legitimate school stuff more than 6 hours per day with no prompting from advisor.	Working on legitimate school stuff more than 6 hours per day, but with prompting to be on task from advisor.	Working Less that 6 hours per day on school stuff.	Off task more often than on. Look for different type of learning environment.
Project Progress	Project credit total is ahead of schedule.	Project credit total is right on schedule.	Project credit total is 1 to 5 credits behind schedule (up to 6 months behind).	Project credit total is more than 5 credits behind schedule (more than 6 months behind).
Helping at School	Student helps with regular chores, and will notice things that need to be done and just do them.	Student eagerly and without excessive prompting helps out with regular chores and cleaning.	Student will do chores, but requires some prompting and will usually grumble along the way.	Student may or may not help with chores. If s/he helps it is with much prompting. S/he just doesn't seem to care.
Appreciation for School	Student is active in showing what MNCS has done for him/her and displays an appreciation for MNCS.	Student understands what MNCS is all about and can see the potential for themselves and others, and that appreciation extends to others.	Student attends school and can see what MNCS could do for them. The respect for education doesn't extend beyond him/her.	Student looks at MNCS as just another school. S/he really doesn't know what MNCS could do for them.
Outside of School	Represents MNCS well when out in the community. Speaks well of MNCS and promotes the school in a positive manner.	Represents MNCS well when out in the community and attempts to promote the school in a positive way.	Displays appropriate behavior when in the community.	Does not represent MNCS well when out in the community (inappropriate language, actions).

PROJECT CHECK LIST

NAME _____ PROJECT_____

PHASE 1
- ❑ Brainstorm ideas—make list
- ❑ Narrow list
- ❑ Pick one (save others for future)
- ❑ What do I/we know?
- ❑ What do I/we want to know?
- ❑ Collect references
- ❑ Complete Web/outline
- ❑ Possible profile learning areas covered
- ❑ Review with peer (friend)
- ❑ Review with parent/guardian/adult friend
- ❑ Review with advisor
- ❑ Review with project planning team
- ❑ Complete documentation of time and learning

PHASE 2
- ❑ Research
- ❑ Take notes
- ❑ Start rough work
- ❑ Collect more references as needed
- ❑ Find and connect with personal information source
- ❑ Complete documentation of time and learning

PHASE 3

- ❏ Complete most (2/3 or more) of rough work
- ❏ Review with peer (friend)
- ❏ Review with parent/guardian/adult friend
- ❏ Review with advisor
- ❏ Review with project planning team
- ❏ Complete documentation of time and learning

PHASE 4

- ❏ Complete rough work
- ❏ Make revisions
- ❏ Review with peer (friend)
- ❏ Review with parent/guardian/adult friend
- ❏ Review with advisor
- ❏ Complete final product
- ❏ Complete documentation of time and learning

PHASE 5

- ❏ Complete reflection thoughts
  - • What went well?
  - • What problems did I encounter?
  - • What did I learn?
- ❏ Complete any final finishing touches
- ❏ Complete project evaluation
- ❏ Plan presentation
- ❏ Practice presentation
- ❏ Complete documentation of time and learning
- ❏ Review
- ❏ Project planning team evaluation

Presentation & Exhibition Evaluation Form for Minnesota New Country School

Student's Name_____ Date_____
Project Title_____ Evaluator_____

Presentation Skills	*Poor*	*Fair*	*Good*	*Excellent*	
Introduces self with poise	1	2	3	4	NA
Identifies project and significance	1	2	3	4	NA
Acknowledges resources and mentors	1	2	3	4	NA
Makes clear what to expect and look for	1	2	3	4	NA
Makes eye contact and speaks to audience	1	2	3	4	NA
Speech is relaxed and conversational	1	2	3	4	NA
Speech is loud enough to hear	1	2	3	4	NA
Uses Standard English, avoids slang, etc.	1	2	3	4	NA

Knowledge & Application Skills					
Provides informative, in-depth history	1	2	3	4	NA
Reveals a high degree of research	1	2	3	4	NA
Reveals a high degree of understanding	1	2	3	4	NA
Provides all correct information necessary	1	2	3	4	NA
Responds clearly and concisely to questions	1	2	3	4	NA

Organization & Problem Solving					
Presentation is organized & easy to follow	1	2	3	4	NA
Production process is explained	1	2	3	4	NA
Provides insight into problems/solutions	1	2	3	4	NA
Promotes understanding of concepts	1	2	3	4	NA
Provides logical closure to the question((s)	1	2	3	4	NA

	Poor	*Fair*	*Good*	*Excellent*	
Display and/or Product					
Demonstrates high level of technology skill	1	2	3	4	NA
Overall physical quality is high	1	2	3	4	NA
Arrangement shows artistry & creativity	1	2	3	4	NA

COMMENTS:

References and Suggested Readings

Buck Institute for Education. (2001). *Project-based learning: An overview.* Found at http:/www.bie.org/pbl/overview/features.html.

Bulkley, K., & Fisler, J. (2002). *A decade of charter schools: From theory to practice.* Consortium for Policy Research in Education policy briefs, April, University of Pennsylvania.

Caine, G., Caine, R., & Crowell, S. (1999). *Mindshifts: A brain-compatible process for professional development and the renewal of education* (2nd ed.). Tucson, AZ: Zephyr Press.

Caine, R., & Caine, G. (1997). *Education on the edge of possibility.* Alexandria, VA: ASCD.

Caine, R., & Caine, G. (1997). *Unleashing the power of perceptual change: The potential of brain-based teaching.* Alexandria, VA: ASCD.

Caine, R., & Caine, G. (1994). *Making connections: Teaching and the human brain.* Menlo Park, CA: Innovative Learning Publications.

Caine, R. N. (2000). Building the bridge from research to classroom. *Educational Leadership, 58*(3).

Cobb, C. D., & Mayer, J. D. (2000). Emotional intelligence: What the research says. *Educational Leadership, 58*(3).

Damasio, A. (1999). *The feeling of what happens: Body and emotion in the making of consciousness.* New York: Harcourt Brace.

Damasio, A. (1994). *Descartes' error: Emotion, reason, and the human brain.* New York: G. P. Putnam's Sons.

D'Arcangelo, M. (2000). The scientist in the crib: A conversation with Andrew Meltzoff. *Educational Leadership, 58*(3).

Dewey, J. (1916). *Democracy and education.* New York: Macmillan.

Dirkswager, E. (Ed.) (2002). *Teachers as owners: A key to revitalizing education.* Lanham, MD: ScarecrowEducation.

Fried, R. (2001). Passionate learners and the challenge of schooling. *Phi Delta Kappan, 83*(2).

Given, B. K. (2000). Theatres of the mind. *Educational Leadership, 58*(3).

Gardner, H. (1999). *The disciplined mind.* New York: Simon & Schuster.

Gardner, H. (1983). *Frames of mind: The theory of multiple intelligences.* New York: Basic Books.

Glickman, C. (1998). *Revolutionizing America's schools.* San Francisco: Jossey-Bass.

Goleman, D. (1995). *Emotional intelligence.* New York: Bantam.

Goodlad, J. (1984). *A place called school.* New York: McGraw-Hill.

Hart, L. A. (2002). *Human brain and human learning* (Rev. Ed.). Kent, WA: Books for Educators.

How people learn: Brain, mind, experience, and school. (1999). National Academy Press.

Jensen, E. (1995). *The learning brain.* San Diego, CA.: The Brain Store.

Jensen, E (2000). Moving with the brain in mind. *Educational Leadership, 58*(3).

Jensen, E. (1998). *Teaching with the brain in mind.* Alexandria, VA: ASCD.

Kovalik, S. (1995). *Integrated thematic instruction: The model.* Kent, WA: Books for Educators.

Levine, E. (2002). *One kid at a time.* New York: Teacher's College Press, Columbia University.

Marzano, R., et al. (1993) *Dimensions of learning teacher's manual* (2nd. ed.). Alexandria, VA: ASCD.

Matthews, D. (1997). *Is there a public for public schools?* Dayton, OH: Kettering Foundation Press.

November, A. (2002). *Creating a new culture of teaching and learning.* Article found at http://anovember.com/articles/asilomar.html.

Palmer, P. (1997). *The courage to teach: Exploring the inner landscape of a teacher's life.* San Francisco: Jossey-Bass.

Pappert, S. (1993). *The children's machine: Rethinking school in the age of the computer.* New York: Basic Books.

Spady, B. (2000). *Beyond counterfeit reforms.* Lanham, MD: Scarecrow Press.

Sylwester, R. (2000a). *A biological brain in a cultural classroom: Applying biological research to classroom management.* Thousand Oaks, CA: Corwin Press.

Sylwester, R. (2000b). Unconscious emotions, conscious feelings. *Educational Leadership, 58*(3).

Sylwester, R. (1995). *A celebration of neurons.* Alexandria, VA: ASCD.

Wagmeister, J., & Shifrin, B. (2000). Thinking differently, learning differently. *Educational Leadership, 58*(3).

Wagner, T. (2001). *Making the grade: Reinventing America's schools.* New York: RoutledgeFalmer.

Wagner, T. (2000). *Bridging the gap between educators and the public.* From a presentation at the Small Schools Workshop. Oakland, CA, February 1–3.

Westwater, A., & Wolfe, P. (2000). The brain-compatible curriculum. *Educational Leadership, 58*(3).

Yoram, H., & Lefstein, A. (2000). Communities of thinking. *Educational Leadership, 58*(3).

Index

About the Author

I am a native Minnesotan and was born and raised "up north" near the Canadian border in the Red River Valley. I lived a Tom Sawyer existence, attending a one-room country school for two years and small schools thereafter, which I'm sure colored my ideas on education. After attending a small high school, I attended St. Olaf College in Northfield, Minnesota. I taught history in a high school in Mapleton (another small school in Minnesota) for twenty-six years thereafter. In 1973 I received a master of science degree in history from Mankato State University and in 1993 I became involved in helping create the Minnesota New Country School in LeSeuer (now in Henderson). After being an advisor at a radically different school, I felt the need to learn even more about learning and felt a desire to help other teachers learn new ways of doing things, so I took a year off to finish my Ed.D. at the University of South Dakota. I worked in teacher preparation departments at Mankato State University and St. Cloud State University, both in Minnesota, from 1996 through 2000.

I decided to leave the "unreformable" state college system and work full-time on radical reforms in 2001. I am presently the learning program director for the Gates-EdVisions Project and a director on the board of EdVisions Cooperative, both of which are committed to developing small, focused, project-based schools that are governed by teachers.

I am married to my wife of 37 years, Caroljean, and have two sons, Lance and Ryan, and one daughter, Monessa.